HBR'S 10 MUST READS

On
Change
Management

On
Change
Management

HARVARD BUSINESS REVIEW PRESS
Boston, Massachusetts

Library of Congress Cataloging-in-Publication Data
HBR's 10 must reads on change management.
       p. cm.
    Includes index.
    ISBN 978-1-4221-5800-5 (pbk. : alk. paper)   1. Organizational change
    2. Leadership   I. Harvard business review   II. Title: HBR's ten must reads
on change management   III. Title: Harvard business review's 10 must reads on
change management.
    HD58.8.H394 2010
    658.4'06—dc22

                                                                2010031616

Contents

On
Change
Management

Leading Change

Why Transformation Efforts Fail. *by John P. Kotter*

OVER THE PAST DECADE, I have watched more than 100 companies try to remake themselves into significantly better competitors. They have included large organizations (Ford) and small ones (Landmark Communications), companies based in the United States (General Motors) and elsewhere (British Airways), corporations that were on their knees (Eastern Airlines), and companies that were earning good money (Bristol-Myers Squibb). These efforts have gone under many banners: total quality management, reengineering, rightsizing, restructuring, cultural change, and turnaround. But, in almost every case, the basic goal has been the same: to make fundamental changes in how business is conducted in order to help cope with a new, more challenging market environment.

A few of these corporate change efforts have been very successful. A few have been utter failures. Most fall somewhere in between, with a distinct tilt toward the lower end of the scale. The lessons that can be drawn are interesting and will probably be relevant to even more organizations in the increasingly competitive business environment of the coming decade.

The most general lesson to be learned from the more successful cases is that the change process goes through a series of phases that, in total, usually require a considerable length of time. Skipping steps creates only the illusion of speed and never produces a satisfying result. A second very general lesson is that critical mistakes in any of the phases can have a devastating impact, slowing momentum and

Eight steps to transforming your organization

1 **Establishing a sense of urgency**
   - Examining market and competitive realities
   - Identifying and discussing crises, potential crises, or major opportunities

2 **Forming a powerful guiding coalition**
   - Assembling a group with enough power to lead the change effort
   - Encouraging the group to work together as a team

3 **Creating a vision**
   - Creating a vision to help direct the change effort
   - Developing strategies for achieving that vision

4 **Communicating the vision**
   - Using every vehicle possible to communicate the new vision and strategies
   - Teaching new behaviors by the example of the guiding coalition

5 **Empowering others to act on the vision**
   - Getting rid of obstacles to change
   - Changing systems or structures that seriously undermine the vision
   - Encouraging risk taking and nontraditional ideas, activities, and actions

6 **Planning for and creating short-term wins**
   - Planning for visible performance improvements
   - Creating those improvements
   - Recognizing and rewarding employees involved in the improvements

7 **Consolidating improvements and producing still more change**
   - Using increased credibility to change systems, structures, and policies that don't fit the vision
   - Hiring, promoting, and developing employees who can implement the vision
   - Reinvigorating the process with new projects, themes, and change agents

8 **Institutionalizing new approaches**
   - Articulating the connections between the new behaviors and corporate success
   - Developing the means to ensure leadership development and succession

Idea in Brief

Most major change initiatives—whether intended to boost quality, improve culture, or reverse a corporate death spiral—generate only lukewarm results. Many fail miserably.

Why? Kotter maintains that too many managers don't realize transformation is a *process*, not an event. It advances through stages that build on each other. And it takes years. Pressured to accelerate the process, managers skip stages. But shortcuts never work.

Equally troubling, even highly capable managers make critical mistakes—such as declaring victory too soon. Result? Loss of momentum, reversal of hard-won gains, and devastation of the entire transformation effort.

By understanding the stages of change—and the pitfalls unique to each stage—you boost your chances of a successful transformation. The payoff? Your organization flexes with tectonic shifts in competitors, markets, and technologies—leaving rivals far behind.

negating hard-won gains. Perhaps because we have relatively little experience in renewing organizations, even very capable people often make at least one big error.

Error 1: Not Establishing a Great Enough Sense of Urgency

Most successful change efforts begin when some individuals or some groups start to look hard at a company's competitive situation, market position, technological trends, and financial performance. They focus on the potential revenue drop when an important patent expires, the five-year trend in declining margins in a core business, or an emerging market that everyone seems to be ignoring. They then find ways to communicate this information broadly and dramatically, especially with respect to crises, potential crises, or great opportunities that are very timely. This first step is essential because just getting a transformation program started requires the aggressive cooperation of many individuals. Without motivation, people won't help, and the effort goes nowhere.

Compared with other steps in the change process, phase one can sound easy. It is not. Well over 50% of the companies I have watched

Idea in Practice

To give your transformation effort the best chance of succeeding, take the right actions at each stage—and avoid common pitfalls

Stage	Actions needed	Pitfalls
Establish a sense of urgency	• Examine market and competitive realities for potential crises and untapped opportunities. • Convince at least 75% of your managers that the status quo is more dangerous than the unknown.	• Underestimating the difficulty of driving people from their comfort zones • Becoming paralyzed by risks
Form a powerful guiding coalition	• Assemble a group with shared commitment and enough power to lead the change effort. • Encourage them to work as a team outside the normal hierarchy.	• No prior experience in teamwork at the top • Relegating team leadership to an HR, quality, or strategic-planning executive rather than a senior line manager
Create a vision	• Create a vision to direct the change effort. • Develop strategies for realizing that vision.	• Presenting a vision that's too complicated or vague to be communicated in five minutes
Communicate the vision	• Use every vehicle possible to communicate the new vision and strategies for achieving it. • Teach new behaviors by the example of the guiding coalition.	• Undercommunicating the vision • Behaving in ways antithetical to the vision

fail in this first phase. What are the reasons for that failure? Sometimes executives underestimate how hard it can be to drive people out of their comfort zones. Sometimes they grossly overestimate how successful they have already been in increasing urgency. Sometimes they lack patience: "Enough with the preliminaries; let's get on with it." In many cases, executives become paralyzed by the downside

Stage	Actions needed	Pitfalls
Empower others to act on the vision	• Remove or alter systems or structures undermining the vision. • Encourage risk taking and nontraditional ideas, activities, and actions.	• Failing to remove powerful individuals who resist the change effort
Plan for and create short-term wins	• Define and engineer visible performance improvements. • Recognize and reward employees contributing to those improvements.	• Leaving short-term successes up to chance • Failing to score successes early enough (12–24 months into the change effort)
Consolidate improvements and produce more change	• Use increased credibility from early wins to change systems, structures, and policies undermining the vision. • Hire, promote, and develop employees who can implement the vision. • Reinvigorate the change process with new projects and change agents.	• Declaring victory too soon—with the first performance improvement • Allowing resistors to convince "troops" that the war has been won
Institutionalize new approaches	• Articulate connections between new behaviors and corporate success. • Create leadership development and succession plans consistent with the new approach.	• Not creating new social norms and shared values consistent with changes • Promoting people into leadership positions who don't personify the new approach

possibilities. They worry that employees with seniority will become defensive, that morale will drop, that events will spin out of control, that short-term business results will be jeopardized, that the stock will sink, and that they will be blamed for creating a crisis.

A paralyzed senior management often comes from having too many managers and not enough leaders. Management's mandate is to minimize risk and to keep the current system operating. Change, by definition, requires creating a new system, which in turn always demands leadership. Phase one in a renewal process typically goes nowhere until enough real leaders are promoted or hired into senior-level jobs.

Transformations often begin, and begin well, when an organization has a new head who is a good leader and who sees the need for a major change. If the renewal target is the entire company, the CEO is key. If change is needed in a division, the division general manager is key. When these individuals are not new leaders, great leaders, or change champions, phase one can be a huge challenge.

Bad business results are both a blessing and a curse in the first phase. On the positive side, losing money does catch people's attention. But it also gives less maneuvering room. With good business results, the opposite is true: Convincing people of the need for change is much harder, but you have more resources to help make changes.

But whether the starting point is good performance or bad, in the more successful cases I have witnessed, an individual or a group always facilitates a frank discussion of potentially unpleasant facts about new competition, shrinking margins, decreasing market share, flat earnings, a lack of revenue growth, or other relevant indices of a declining competitive position. Because there seems to be an almost universal human tendency to shoot the bearer of bad news, especially if the head of the organization is not a change champion, executives in these companies often rely on outsiders to bring unwanted information. Wall Street analysts, customers, and consultants can all be helpful in this regard. The purpose of all this activity, in the words of one former CEO of a large European company, is "to make the status quo seem more dangerous than launching into the unknown."

In a few of the most successful cases, a group has manufactured a crisis. One CEO deliberately engineered the largest accounting loss in the company's history, creating huge pressures from Wall Street in the process. One division president commissioned first-ever customer satisfaction surveys, knowing full well that the results would be terrible. He then made these findings public. On the surface, such moves can look unduly risky. But there is also risk in playing it too safe: When the urgency rate is not pumped up enough, the transformation process cannot succeed, and the long-term future of the organization is put in jeopardy.

When is the urgency rate high enough? From what I have seen, the answer is when about 75% of a company's management is honestly convinced that business as usual is totally unacceptable. Anything less can produce very serious problems later on in the process.

Error 2: Not Creating a Powerful Enough Guiding Coalition

Major renewal programs often start with just one or two people. In cases of successful transformation efforts, the leadership coalition grows and grows over time. But whenever some minimum mass is not achieved early in the effort, nothing much worthwhile happens.

It is often said that major change is impossible unless the head of the organization is an active supporter. What I am talking about goes far beyond that. In successful transformations, the chairman or president or division general manager, plus another five or 15 or 50 people, come together and develop a shared commitment to excellent performance through renewal. In my experience, this group never includes all of the company's most senior executives because some people just won't buy in, at least not at first. But in the most successful cases, the coalition is always pretty powerful—in terms of titles, information and expertise, reputations, and relationships.

In both small and large organizations, a successful guiding team may consist of only three to five people during the first year of a renewal effort. But in big companies, the coalition needs to grow to the 20 to 50 range before much progress can be made in phase three and beyond. Senior managers always form the core of the group. But sometimes you find board members, a representative from a key customer, or even a powerful union leader.

Because the guiding coalition includes members who are not part of senior management, it tends to operate outside of the normal hierarchy by definition. This can be awkward, but it is clearly necessary. If the existing hierarchy were working well, there would be no need for a major transformation. But since the current system is not working, reform generally demands activity outside of formal boundaries, expectations, and protocol.

A high sense of urgency within the managerial ranks helps enormously in putting a guiding coalition together. But more is usually required. Someone needs to get these people together, help them develop a shared assessment of their company's problems and opportunities, and create a minimum level of trust and communication. Off-site retreats, for two or three days, are one popular vehicle for accomplishing this task. I have seen many groups of five to 35 executives attend a series of these retreats over a period of months.

Companies that fail in phase two usually underestimate the difficulties of producing change and thus the importance of a powerful guiding coalition. Sometimes they have no history of teamwork at the top and therefore undervalue the importance of this type of coalition. Sometimes they expect the team to be led by a staff executive from human resources, quality, or strategic planning instead of a key line manager. No matter how capable or dedicated the staff head, groups without strong line leadership never achieve the power that is required.

Efforts that don't have a powerful enough guiding coalition can make apparent progress for a while. But, sooner or later, the opposition gathers itself together and stops the change.

Error 3: Lacking a Vision

In every successful transformation effort that I have seen, the guiding coalition develops a picture of the future that is relatively easy to communicate and appeals to customers, stockholders, and employees. A vision always goes beyond the numbers that are typically found in five-year plans. A vision says something that helps clarify the direction in which an organization needs to move. Sometimes the first draft comes mostly from a single individual. It is usually a bit blurry, at least initially. But after the coalition works at it for three or five or even 12 months, something much better emerges through their tough analytical thinking and a little dreaming. Eventually, a strategy for achieving that vision is also developed.

In one midsize European company, the first pass at a vision contained two-thirds of the basic ideas that were in the final product. The concept of global reach was in the initial version from the beginning. So was the idea of becoming preeminent in certain businesses. But one central idea in the final version—getting out of low value-added activities—came only after a series of discussions over a period of several months.

Without a sensible vision, a transformation effort can easily dissolve into a list of confusing and incompatible projects that can take the organization in the wrong direction or nowhere at all. Without a sound vision, the reengineering project in the accounting department, the new 360-degree performance appraisal from the human resources department, the plant's quality program, the cultural change project in the sales force will not add up in a meaningful way.

In failed transformations, you often find plenty of plans, directives, and programs but no vision. In one case, a company gave out four-inch-thick notebooks describing its change effort. In mind-numbing detail, the books spelled out procedures, goals, methods, and deadlines. But nowhere was there a clear and compelling statement of where all this was leading. Not surprisingly, most of the employees with whom I talked were either confused or alienated. The big, thick books did not rally them together or inspire change. In fact, they probably had just the opposite effect.

In a few of the less successful cases that I have seen, management had a sense of direction, but it was too complicated or blurry to be useful. Recently, I asked an executive in a midsize company to describe his vision and received in return a barely comprehensible 30-minute lecture. Buried in his answer were the basic elements of a sound vision. But they were buried—deeply.

A useful rule of thumb: If you can't communicate the vision to someone in five minutes or less and get a reaction that signifies both understanding and interest, you are not yet done with this phase of the transformation process.

Error 4: Undercommunicating the Vision by a Factor of Ten

I've seen three patterns with respect to communication, all very common. In the first, a group actually does develop a pretty good transformation vision and then proceeds to communicate it by holding a single meeting or sending out a single communication. Having used about 0.0001% of the yearly intracompany communication, the group is startled when few people seem to understand the new approach. In the second pattern, the head of the organization spends a considerable amount of time making speeches to employee groups, but most people still don't get it (not surprising, since vision captures only 0.0005% of the total yearly communication). In the third pattern, much more effort goes into newsletters and speeches, but some very visible senior executives still behave in ways that are antithetical to the vision. The net result is that cynicism among the troops goes up, while belief in the communication goes down.

Transformation is impossible unless hundreds or thousands of people are willing to help, often to the point of making short-term sacrifices. Employees will not make sacrifices, even if they are unhappy with the status quo, unless they believe that useful change is possible. Without credible communication, and a lot of it, the hearts and minds of the troops are never captured.

This fourth phase is particularly challenging if the short-term sacrifices include job losses. Gaining understanding and support is tough when downsizing is a part of the vision. For this reason, successful visions usually include new growth possibilities and the commitment to treat fairly anyone who is laid off.

Executives who communicate well incorporate messages into their hour-by-hour activities. In a routine discussion about a business problem, they talk about how proposed solutions fit (or don't fit) into the bigger picture. In a regular performance appraisal, they talk about how the employee's behavior helps or undermines the vision. In a review of a division's quarterly performance, they talk not only about the numbers but also about how the division's executives are contributing to the transformation. In a routine Q&A with employees at a company facility, they tie their answers back to renewal goals.

In more successful transformation efforts, executives use all existing communication channels to broadcast the vision. They turn boring, unread company newsletters into lively articles about the vision. They take ritualistic, tedious quarterly management meetings and turn them into exciting discussions of the transformation. They throw out much of the company's generic management education and replace it with courses that focus on business problems and the new vision. The guiding principle is simple: Use every possible channel, especially those that are being wasted on nonessential information.

Perhaps even more important, most of the executives I have known in successful cases of major change learn to "walk the talk." They consciously attempt to become a living symbol of the new corporate culture. This is often not easy. A 60-year-old plant manager who has spent precious little time over 40 years thinking about customers will not suddenly behave in a customer-oriented way. But I have witnessed just such a person change, and change a great deal. In that case, a high level of urgency helped. The fact that the man was a part of the guiding coalition and the vision-creation team also helped. So did all the communication, which kept reminding him of the desired behavior, and all the feedback from his peers and subordinates, which helped him see when he was not engaging in that behavior.

Communication comes in both words and deeds, and the latter are often the most powerful form. Nothing undermines change more than behavior by important individuals that is inconsistent with their words.

Error 5: Not Removing Obstacles to the New Vision

Successful transformations begin to involve large numbers of people as the process progresses. Employees are emboldened to try new approaches, to develop new ideas, and to provide leadership. The only constraint is that the actions fit within the broad parameters of the overall vision. The more people involved, the better the outcome.

To some degree, a guiding coalition empowers others to take action simply by successfully communicating the new direction. But communication is never sufficient by itself. Renewal also requires the removal of obstacles. Too often, an employee understands the new vision and wants to help make it happen, but an elephant appears to be blocking the path. In some cases, the elephant is in the person's head, and the challenge is to convince the individual that no external obstacle exists. But in most cases, the blockers are very real.

Sometimes the obstacle is the organizational structure: Narrow job categories can seriously undermine efforts to increase productivity or make it very difficult even to think about customers. Sometimes compensation or performance-appraisal systems make people choose between the new vision and their own self-interest. Perhaps worst of all are bosses who refuse to change and who make demands that are inconsistent with the overall effort.

One company began its transformation process with much publicity and actually made good progress through the fourth phase. Then the change effort ground to a halt because the officer in charge of the company's largest division was allowed to undermine most of the new initiatives. He paid lip service to the process but did not change his behavior or encourage his managers to change. He did not reward the unconventional ideas called for in the vision. He allowed human resource systems to remain intact even when they were clearly inconsistent with the new ideals. I think the officer's motives were complex. To some degree, he did not believe the company needed major change. To some degree, he felt personally threatened by all the change. To some degree, he was afraid that he could not produce both change and the expected operating profit. But despite the fact that they backed the renewal effort, the other officers did virtually nothing to stop the one blocker. Again, the reasons were complex. The company had no history of confronting problems like this. Some people were afraid of the officer. The CEO was concerned that he might lose a talented executive. The net result was disastrous. Lower-level managers concluded that senior management had lied to them about their commitment to renewal, cynicism grew, and the whole effort collapsed.

In the first half of a transformation, no organization has the momentum, power, or time to get rid of all obstacles. But the big ones must be confronted and removed. If the blocker is a person, it is important that he or she be treated fairly and in a way that is consistent with the new vision. Action is essential, both to empower others and to maintain the credibility of the change effort as a whole.

Error 6: Not Systematically Planning for, and Creating, Short-Term Wins

Real transformation takes time, and a renewal effort risks losing momentum if there are no short-term goals to meet and celebrate. Most people won't go on the long march unless they see compelling evidence in 12 to 24 months that the journey is producing expected results. Without short-term wins, too many people give up or actively join the ranks of those people who have been resisting change.

One to two years into a successful transformation effort, you find quality beginning to go up on certain indices or the decline in net income stopping. You find some successful new product introductions or an upward shift in market share. You find an impressive productivity improvement or a statistically higher customer satisfaction rating. But whatever the case, the win is unambiguous. The result is not just a judgment call that can be discounted by those opposing change.

Creating short-term wins is different from hoping for short-term wins. The latter is passive, the former active. In a successful transformation, managers actively look for ways to obtain clear performance improvements, establish goals in the yearly planning system, achieve the objectives, and reward the people involved with recognition, promotions, and even money. For example, the guiding coalition at a U.S. manufacturing company produced a highly visible and successful new product introduction about 20 months after the start of its renewal effort. The new product was selected about six months into the effort because it met multiple criteria: It could be designed and launched in a relatively short period, it could be handled by a small team of people who were devoted to the new vision, it had upside potential, and the new product-development team could operate outside the established departmental structure without practical problems. Little was left to chance, and the win boosted the credibility of the renewal process.

Managers often complain about being forced to produce short-term wins, but I've found that pressure can be a useful element in a change effort. When it becomes clear to people that major change will take a long time, urgency levels can drop. Commitments to produce short-term wins help keep the urgency level up and force detailed analytical thinking that can clarify or revise visions.

Error 7: Declaring Victory Too Soon

After a few years of hard work, managers may be tempted to declare victory with the first clear performance improvement. While celebrating a win is fine, declaring the war won can be catastrophic. Until changes sink deeply into a company's culture, a process that can take five to ten years, new approaches are fragile and subject to regression.

In the recent past, I have watched a dozen change efforts operate under the reengineering theme. In all but two cases, victory was declared and the expensive consultants were paid and thanked when the first major project was completed after two to three years. Within two more years, the useful changes that had been introduced slowly disappeared. In two of the ten cases, it's hard to find any trace of the reengineering work today.

Over the past 20 years, I've seen the same sort of thing happen to huge quality projects, organizational development efforts, and more. Typically, the problems start early in the process: The urgency level is not intense enough, the guiding coalition is not powerful enough, and the vision is not clear enough. But it is the premature victory celebration that kills momentum. And then the powerful forces associated with tradition take over.

Ironically, it is often a combination of change initiators and change resistors that creates the premature victory celebration. In their enthusiasm over a clear sign of progress, the initiators go overboard. They are then joined by resistors, who are quick to spot any opportunity to stop change. After the celebration is over, the resistors point to the victory as a sign that the war has been won and the troops should be sent home. Weary troops allow themselves to be convinced that they won. Once home, the foot soldiers are reluctant to climb back on the ships. Soon thereafter, change comes to a halt, and tradition creeps back in.

Instead of declaring victory, leaders of successful efforts use the credibility afforded by short-term wins to tackle even bigger problems. They go after systems and structures that are not consistent with the transformation vision and have not been confronted before. They pay great attention to who is promoted, who is hired, and how people are developed. They include new reengineering projects that are even bigger in scope than the initial ones. They understand that renewal efforts take not months but years. In fact, in one of the most successful transformations that I have ever seen, we quantified the amount of change that occurred each year over a seven-year period. On a scale of one (low) to ten (high), year one received a two, year two a four, year three a three, year four a seven, year five an eight, year six a four, and year seven a two. The peak came in year five, fully 36 months after the first set of visible wins.

Error 8: Not Anchoring Changes in the Corporation's Culture

In the final analysis, change sticks when it becomes "the way we do things around here," when it seeps into the bloodstream of the corporate body. Until new behaviors are rooted in social norms and shared values, they are subject to degradation as soon as the pressure for change is removed.

Two factors are particularly important in institutionalizing change in corporate culture. The first is a conscious attempt to show people how the new approaches, behaviors, and attitudes have helped improve performance. When people are left on their own to make the connections, they sometimes create very inaccurate links. For example, because results improved while charismatic Harry was boss, the troops link his mostly idiosyncratic style with those results instead of seeing how their own improved customer service and productivity were instrumental. Helping people see the right connections requires communication. Indeed, one company was relentless, and it paid off enormously. Time was spent at every major management meeting to discuss why performance was increasing. The company newspaper ran article after article showing how changes had boosted earnings.

The second factor is taking sufficient time to make sure that the next generation of top management really does personify the new approach. If the requirements for promotion don't change, renewal rarely lasts. One bad succession decision at the top of an organization can undermine a decade of hard work. Poor succession decisions are possible when boards of directors are not an integral part of the renewal effort. In at least three instances I have seen, the champion for change was the retiring executive, and although his successor was not a resistor, he was not a change champion. Because the boards did not understand the transformations in any detail, they could not see that their choices were not good fits. The retiring executive in one case tried unsuccessfully to talk his board into a less seasoned candidate who better personified the transformation. In the other two cases, the CEOs did not resist the boards' choices, because they felt the transformation could not be undone by their successors. They were wrong. Within two years, signs of renewal began to disappear at both companies.

There are still more mistakes that people make, but these eight are the big ones. I realize that in a short article everything is made to sound a bit too simplistic. In reality, even successful change efforts are messy and full of surprises. But just as a relatively simple vision is needed to guide people through a major change, so a vision of the change process can reduce the error rate. And fewer errors can spell the difference between success and failure.

Originally published March 1995. Reprint R0701J

Change Through Persuasion

by David A. Garvin and Michael A. Roberto

FACED WITH THE NEED for massive change, most managers respond predictably. They revamp the organization's strategy, then round up the usual set of suspects—people, pay, and processes—shifting around staff, realigning incentives, and rooting out inefficiencies. They then wait patiently for performance to improve, only to be bitterly disappointed. For some reason, the right things still don't happen.

Why is change so hard? First of all, most people are reluctant to alter their habits. What worked in the past is good enough; in the absence of a dire threat, employees will keep doing what they've always done. And when an organization has had a succession of leaders, resistance to change is even stronger. A legacy of disappointment and distrust creates an environment in which employees automatically condemn the next turnaround champion to failure, assuming that he or she is "just like all the others." Calls for sacrifice and self-discipline are met with cynicism, skepticism, and knee-jerk resistance.

Our research into organizational transformation has involved settings as diverse as multinational corporations, government agencies, nonprofits, and high-performing teams like mountaineering expeditions and firefighting crews. We've found that for change to stick, leaders must design and run an effective persuasion campaign—one that begins weeks or months before the actual turnaround plan is set in concrete. Managers must perform significant work up front to ensure that employees will actually listen to tough messages, question old assumptions, and consider new ways of working. This means taking a series of deliberate but subtle steps to recast employees' prevailing views and create a new context for action. Such a shaping process must be actively managed during the first few months of a turnaround, when uncertainty is high and setbacks are inevitable. Otherwise, there is little hope for sustained improvement.

Like a political campaign, a persuasion campaign is largely one of differentiation from the past. To the typical change-averse employee, all restructuring plans look alike. The trick for turnaround leaders is to show employees precisely how their plans differ from their predecessors'. They must convince people that the organization is truly on its deathbed—or, at the very least, that radical changes are required if it is to survive and thrive. (This is a particularly difficult challenge when years of persistent problems have been accompanied by few changes in the status quo.) Turnaround leaders must also gain trust by demonstrating through word and deed that they are the right leaders for the job and must convince employees that theirs is the correct plan for moving forward.

Accomplishing all this calls for a four-part communications strategy. Prior to announcing a policy or issuing a set of instructions, leaders need to set the stage for acceptance. At the time of delivery, they must create the frame through which information and messages are interpreted. As time passes, they must manage the mood so that employees' emotional states support implementation and follow-through. And at critical intervals, they must provide reinforcement to ensure that the desired changes take hold without backsliding.

In this article, we describe this process in more detail, drawing on the example of the turnaround of Beth Israel Deaconess Medical Center (BIDMC) in Boston. Paul Levy, who became CEO in early 2002, managed to bring the failing hospital back from the brink of ruin. We had ringside seats during the first six months of the turnaround. Levy agreed to hold videotaped interviews with us every two to four weeks during that period as we prepared a case study describing his

Idea in Brief

When a company is teetering on the brink of ruin, most turnaround leaders revamp strategy, shift around staff, and root out inefficiencies. Then they wait patiently for the payoff—only to suffer bitter disappointment as the expected improvements fail to materialize.

How to make change stick? Conduct a four-stage persuasion campaign: 1) Prepare your organization's cultural "soil" months before setting your turnaround plan in concrete—by convincing employees that your company can survive only through radical change. 2) Present your plan—explaining in detail its purpose and expected impact. 3) After executing the plan, manage employees' emotions by acknowledging the pain of change—while keeping people focused on the hard work ahead. 4) As the turnaround starts generating results, reinforce desired behavioral changes to prevent backsliding.

Using this four-part process, the CEO of Beth Israel Deaconess Medical Center (BIDMC) brought the failing hospital back from near-certain death. Hemorrhaging $58 million in losses in 2001, BIDMC reported a $37.4 million net gain from operations in 2004. Revenues rose, while costs shrank. Morale soared—as reflected by a drop in nursing turnover from between 15% and 16% in 2002 to just 3% by 2004.

efforts. He also gave us access to his daily calendar, as well as to assorted e-mail correspondence and internal memorandums and reports. From this wealth of data, we were able to track the change process as it unfolded, without the usual biases and distortions that come from 20/20 hindsight. The story of how Levy tilled the soil for change provides lessons for any CEO in a turnaround situation.

Setting the Stage

Paul Levy was an unlikely candidate to run BIDMC. He was not a doctor and had never managed a hospital, though he had previously served as the executive dean for administration at Harvard Medical School. His claim to fame was his role as the architect of the Boston Harbor Cleanup, a multibillion-dollar pollution-control project that

Idea in Practice

Use these steps to persuade your workforce to embrace and execute needed change:

Set the Stage for Acceptance

Develop a bold message that provides compelling reasons to do things differently.

> **Example:** On his first day as Beth Israel Deaconess Medical Center's CEO, Paul Levy publicized the possibility that BIDMC would be sold to a for-profit institution. He delivered an all-hands-on-deck e-mail to the staff citing the hospital's achievements while confirming that the threat of sale was real. The e-mail also signaled actions he would take, including layoffs, and described his open management style (hallway chats, lunches with staff). In addition, Levy circulated a third-party, warts-and-all report on BIDMC's plight on the hospital's intranet—so staff could no longer claim ignorance.

Frame the Turnaround Plan

Present your turnaround plan in a way that helps people interpret your ideas correctly.

> **Example:** Levy augmented his several-hundred-page plan with an e-mail that evoked BIDMC's mission and uncompromising values and reaffirmed the importance of remaining an academic medical center. He provided further details about the plan, emphasizing needed tough measures based on the third-party report. He also explained past plans' deficiencies, contrasting earlier efforts'

he had led several years earlier. (Based on this experience, Levy identified a common yet insidiously destructive organizational dynamic that causes dedicated teams to operate in counterproductive ways, which he described in "The Nut Island Effect: When Good Teams Go Wrong," March 2001.) Six years after completing the Boston Harbor project, Levy approached the BIDMC board and applied for the job of cleaning up the troubled hospital.

Despite his lack of hospital management experience, Levy was appealing to the board. The Boston Harbor Cleanup was a difficult, highly visible change effort that required deft political and managerial skills. Levy had stood firm in the face of tough negotiations and often-heated public resistance and had instilled accountability in top-down methods with his plan's collaborative approach. Employees thus felt the plan belonged to them.

Manage the Mood

Strike the right notes of optimism and realism to make employees feel cared for while also keeping them focused on your plan's execution.

Example: Levy acknowledged the pain of layoffs, then urged employees to look forward to "[setting] an example for what a unique academic medical center like ours means for this region." He also issued progress updates while reminding people that BIDMC still needed to control costs. As financial performance picked up, he lavishly praised the staff.

Prevent Backsliding

Provide opportunities for employees to practice desired behaviors repeatedly. If necessary, publicly criticize disruptive, divisive behaviors.

Example: Levy had established meeting rules requiring staff to state their objections to decisions and to "disagree without being disagreeable." When one medical chief e-mailed Levy complaining about a decision made during a meeting—and copied the other chiefs and board chairman—Levy took action. He responded with an e-mail to the same audience, publicly reprimanding the chief for his tone, lack of civility, and failure to follow the rule about speaking up during meetings.

city and state agencies. He was also a known quantity to the board, having served on a BIDMC steering committee formed by the board chairman in 2001.

Levy saw the prospective job as one of public service. BIDMC was the product of a difficult 1996 merger between two hospitals—Beth Israel and Deaconess—each of which had distinguished reputations, several best-in-the-world departments and specializations, and deeply devoted staffs. The problems began after the merger. A misguided focus on clinical practice rather than backroom integration, a failure to cut costs, and the repeated inability to execute plans and adapt to changing conditions in the health care marketplace all contributed to BIDMC's dismal performance.

By the time the board settled on Levy, affairs at BIDMC had reached the nadir. The hospital was losing $50 million a year. Relations between the administration and medical staff were strained, as were those between management and the board of directors. Employees felt demoralized, having witnessed the rapid decline in their institution's once-legendary status and the disappointing failure of its past leaders. A critical study was conducted by the Hunter Group, a leading health-care consulting firm. The report, detailing the dire conditions at the hospital and the changes needed to turn things around, had been completed but not yet released. Meanwhile, the state attorney general, who was responsible for overseeing charitable trusts, had put pressure on the board to sell the failing BIDMC to a for-profit institution.

Like many CEOs recruited to fix a difficult situation, Levy's first task was to gain a mandate for the changes ahead. He also recognized that crucial negotiations were best conducted before he took the job, when his leverage was greatest, rather than after taking the reins. In particular, he moved to secure the cooperation of the hospital board by flatly stating his conditions for employment. He told the directors, for example, that should they hire him, they could no longer interfere in day-to-day management decisions. In his second and third meetings with the board's search committee, Levy laid out his timetable and intentions. He insisted that the board decide on his appointment quickly so that he could be on the job before the release of the Hunter report. He told the committee that he intended to push for a smaller, more effective group of directors. Though the conditions were somewhat unusual, the board was convinced that Levy had the experience to lead a successful turnaround, and they accepted his terms. Levy went to work on January 7, 2002.

The next task was to set the stage with the hospital staff. Levy was convinced that the employees, hungry for a turnaround, would do their best to cooperate with him if he could emulate and embody the core values of the hospital culture, rather than impose his personal values. He chose to act as the managerial equivalent of a

The four phases of a persuasion campaign

A typical turnaround process consists of two stark phases: plan development, followed by an implementation that may or may not be welcomed by the organization. For the turnaround plan to be widely accepted and adopted, however, the CEO must develop a separate persuasion campaign, the goal of which is to create a continuously receptive environment for change. The campaign begins well before the CEO's first day on the job—or, if the CEO is long established, well before formal development work begins—and continues long after the final plan is announced.

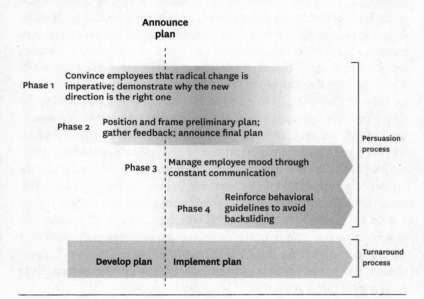

good doctor—that is, as one who, in dealing with a very ill patient, delivers both the bad news and the chances of success honestly and imparts a realistic sense of hope, without sugar coating.

Like any leader facing a turnaround, Levy also knew he had to develop a bold message that provided compelling reasons to do things differently and then cast that message in capital letters to signal the arrival of a new order. To give his message teeth, he linked it to an implicit threat. Taking his cue from his private discussions with the state attorney general, whom he had persuaded to keep the hospital open for the time being, Levy chose to publicize the very real possibility the hospital would be sold. While he realized he risked frightening the staff and the patients with this bad news, he believed that a strong wake-up call was necessary to get employees to face up to the situation.

During his first morning on the job, Levy delivered an all-hands-on-deck e-mail to the staff. The memo contained four broad messages. It opened with the good news, pointing out that the organization had much to be proud of ("This is a wonderful institution, representing the very best in academic medicine: exemplary patient care, extraordinary research, and fine teaching"). Second, Levy noted that the threat of sale was real ("This is our last chance"). Third, he signaled the kinds of actions employees could expect him to take ("There will be a reduction in staff"). And finally, he described the open management style he would adopt. He would manage by walking around—lunching with staff in the cafeteria, having impromptu conversations in the hallways, talking with employees at every opportunity to discover their concerns. He would communicate directly with employees through e-mail rather than through intermediaries. He also noted that the Hunter report would be posted on the hospital intranet, where all employees would have the opportunity to review its recommendations and submit comments for the final turnaround plan. The direct, open tone of the e-mail memo signaled exactly how Levy's management style would differ from that of his predecessors.

In the afternoon, he disclosed BIDMC's situation in interviews with the *Boston Globe* and the *Boston Herald,* the city's two major newspapers. He told reporters the same thing he had told the hospital's employees: that, in the absence of a turnaround, the hospital would be sold to a for-profit chain and would therefore lose its status as a Harvard teaching hospital. Staving off a sale would require tough measures, including the laying off of anywhere from 500 to 700 employees. Levy insisted that there would be no nursing layoffs, in keeping with the hospital's core values of high-quality patient care. The newspaper reports, together with the memo circulated that morning, served to immediately reset employee expectations while dramatically increasing staff cooperation and willingness to accept whatever new initiatives might prove necessary to the hospital's survival.

Two days later, the critical Hunter report came out and was circulated via the hospital's intranet. Because the report had been produced by an objective third party, employees were open to its unvarnished, warts-and-all view of the hospital's current predicament. The facts were stark, and the staff could no longer claim ignorance. Levy received, and personally responded to, more than 300 e-mail suggestions for improvement in response to the report, many of which he later included in the turnaround plan.

Creating the Frame

Once the stage has been set for acceptance, effective leaders need to help employees interpret proposals for change. Complex plans can be interpreted in any number of ways; not all of them ensure acceptance and favorable outcomes. Skilled leaders therefore use "frames" to provide context and shape perspective for new proposals and plans. By framing the issues, leaders help people digest ideas in particular ways. A frame can take many forms: It can be a company-wide presentation that prepares employees before an unexpected change, for example, or a radio interview that provides context following an unsettling layoff.

Levy used one particularly effective framing device to help employees interpret a preliminary draft of the turnaround plan. This device took the form of a detailed e-mail memo accompanying the dense, several-hundred-page plan. The memo explained, in considerable detail, the plan's purpose and expected impact.

The first section of the memo sought to mollify critics and reduce the fears of doctors and nurses. Its tone was positive and uplifting; it discussed BIDMC's mission, strategy, and uncompromising values, emphasizing the hospital's "warm, caring environment." This section of the letter also reaffirmed the importance of remaining an academic medical center, as well as reminding employees of their shared mission and ideals. The second part of the letter told employees what to expect, providing further details about the turnaround plan. It emphasized that tough measures and goals would be required but noted that the specific recommendations were based, for the most part, on the advice in the Hunter report, which employees had already reviewed. The message to employees was, "You've already seen and endorsed the Hunter report. There are no future surprises."

The third part of the letter anticipated and responded to prospective concerns; this had the effect of circumventing objections. This section explicitly diagnosed past plans and explained their deficiencies, which were largely due to their having been imposed top-down, with little employee ownership, buy-in, or discussion. Levy then offered a direct interpretation of what had gone wrong. Past plans, he said, had underestimated the size of the financial problem, set unrealistic expectations for new revenue growth, and failed to test implementation proposals. This section of the letter also drove home the need for change at a deeper, more visceral level than employees had experienced in the past. It emphasized that this plan was a far more collective effort than past proposals had been, because it incorporated many employee suggestions.

By framing the turnaround proposal this way, Levy accomplished two things. First, he was able to convince employees that the plan belonged to them. Second, the letter served as the basis for an ongoing communication platform. Levy reiterated its points at every opportunity—not only with employees but also in public meetings and in discussions with the press.

Managing the Mood

Turnarounds are depressing events, especially when they involve restructuring and downsizing. Relationships are disrupted, friends move on, and jobs disappear. In such settings, managing the mood of the organization becomes an essential leadership skill. Leaders must pay close attention to employees' emotions—the ebb and flow of their feelings and moods—and work hard to preserve a receptive climate for change. Often, this requires a delicate balancing act between presenting good and bad news in just the right proportion. Employees need to feel that their sacrifices have not been in vain and that their accomplishments have been recognized and rewarded. At the same time, they must be reminded that complacency is not an option. The communication challenge is daunting. One must strike the right notes of optimism and realism and carefully calibrate the timing, tone, and positioning of every message.

Paul Levy's challenge was threefold: to give remaining employees time to grieve and recover from layoffs and other difficult measures; to make them feel that he cared for and supported them; and to ensure that the turnaround plan proceeded apace. The process depended on mutual trust and employees' desire to succeed. "I had to calibrate the push and pull of congratulations and pressure, but I also depended on the staff's underlying value system and sense of mission," he said. "They were highly motivated, caring individuals who had stuck with the place through five years of hell. They wanted to do good."

The first step was to acknowledge employees' feelings of depression while helping them look to the future. Immediately after the first round of layoffs, people were feeling listless and dejected; Levy knew that releasing the final version of the turnaround plan too soon after the layoffs could be seen as cold. In an e-mail he sent to all employees a few days later, Levy explicitly empathized with employees' feelings ("This week is a sad one . . . it is hard for those of us remaining . . . offices are emptier than usual"). He then urged employees to look forward and concluded on a strongly optimistic note (". . . our target is not just survival: It is to thrive and set an example for what a unique academic medical center like ours means for this region"). His upbeat words were reinforced by a piece of good luck that weekend when the underdog New England Patriots won their first Super Bowl championship in dramatic fashion in the last 90 seconds of the game. When Levy returned to work the following Monday, employees were saying, "If the Patriots can do it, we can, too."

Dysfunctional Routines

Six Ways to Stop Change in Its Tracks

Just as people are creatures of habit, organizations thrive on routines. Management teams, for example, routinely cut budgets after performance deviates from plan. Routines—predictable, virtually automatic behaviors—are unstated, self-reinforcing, and remarkably resilient. Because they lead to more efficient cognitive processing, they are, for the most part, functional and highly desirable.

A culture of "no"

In organizations dominated by cynics and critics, there is always a good reason not to do something. Piling on criticism is an easy way to avoid taking risks and claim false superiority. Lou Gerstner gets credit for naming this routine, which he found on his arrival at IBM, but it is common in many organizations. Another CEO described her team's response to new initiatives by likening it to a skeet shoot: "Someone would yell, 'Pull!' there would be a deafening blast, and the idea would be in pieces on the ground." This routine has two sources: a culture that overvalues criticism and analysis, and complex decision-making processes requiring multiple approvals, in which anybody can say "no" but nobody can say "yes." It is especially likely in organizations that are divided into large subunits or segments, led by local leaders with great power who are often unwilling to comply with directives from above.

The dog and pony show must go on

Some organizations put so much weight on process that they confuse ends and means, form and content. How you present a proposal becomes more important than what you propose. Managers construct presentations carefully and devote large amounts of time to obtaining sign-offs. The result is death by PowerPoint. Despite the appearance of progress, there's little real headway.

The grass is always greener

To avoid facing challenges in their core business, some managers look to new products, new services, and new lines of business. At times, such diversification is healthy. But all too often these efforts are merely an avoidance tactic that keeps tough problems at arm's length.

The next task was to keep employees focused on the continuing hard work ahead. On April 12, two months into the restructuring process, Levy sent out a "Frequently Asked Questions" e-mail giving a generally favorable view of progress to date. At the same time, he spoke plainly about the need to control costs and reminded employees that merit pay increases would remain on hold. This was hardly the rosy picture that most employees were hoping for, of course. But

Dysfunctional routines, by contrast, are barriers to action and change. Some are outdated behaviors that were appropriate once but are now unhelpful. Others manifest themselves in knee-jerk reactions, passivity, unproductive foot-dragging, and, sometimes, active resistance.

Dysfunctional routines are persistent, but they are not unchangeable. Novelty—the perception that current circumstances are truly different from those that previously prevailed—is one of the most potent forces for dislodging routines. To overcome them, leaders must clearly signal that the context has changed. They must work directly with employees to recognize and publicly examine dysfunctional routines and substitute desired behaviors.

<table>
<tr><td>

After the meeting ends, debate begins

This routine is often hard to spot because so much of it takes place under cover. Cordial, apparently cooperative meetings are followed by resistance. Sometimes, resisters are covert; often, they end-run established forums entirely and take their concerns directly to the top. The result? Politics triumphs over substance, staff meetings become empty rituals, and meddling becomes the norm.

</td><td>

Ready, aim, aim. . .

Here, the problem is the organization's inability to settle on a definitive course of action. Staff members generate a continual stream of proposals and reports; managers repeatedly tinker with each one, fine tuning their choices without ever making a final decision. Often called "analysis paralysis," this pattern is common in perfectionist cultures where mistakes are career threatening and people who rock the boat drown.

</td></tr>
</table>

This too shall pass

In organizations where prior leaders repeatedly proclaimed a state of crisis but then made few substantive changes, employees tend to be jaded. In such situations, they develop a heads-down, bunker mentality and a reluctance to respond to management directives. Most believe that the wisest course of action is to ignore new initiatives, work around them, or wait things out.

Levy believed sufficient time had passed that employees could accommodate a more realistic and tough tone on his part.

A month later, everything changed. Operational improvements that were put in place during the first phase of the turnaround had begun to take hold. Financial performance was well ahead of budget, with the best results since the merger. In another e-mail, Levy praised employees lavishly. He also convened a series of open question-and-answer forums, where employees heard more details about the hospital's tangible progress and received kudos for their accomplishments.

Reinforcing Good Habits

Without a doubt, the toughest challenge faced by leaders during a turnaround is to avoid backsliding into dysfunctional routines— habitual patterns of negative behavior by individuals and groups that are triggered automatically and unconsciously by familiar circumstances or stimuli. (For more on how such disruptive patterns work, see the sidebar "Dysfunctional Routines: Six Ways to Stop Change in Its Tracks.") Employees need help maintaining new behaviors, especially when their old ways of working are deeply ingrained and destructive. Effective change leaders provide opportunities for employees to practice desired behaviors repeatedly, while personally modeling new ways of working and providing coaching and support.

In our studies of successful turnarounds, we've found that effective leaders explicitly reinforce organizational values on a constant basis, using actions to back up their words. Their goal is to change behavior, not just ways of thinking. For example, a leader can talk about values such as openness, tolerance, civility, teamwork, delegation, and direct communication in meetings and e-mails. But the message takes hold only if he or she also signals a dislike of disruptive, divisive behaviors by pointedly—and, if necessary, publicly—criticizing them.

At Beth Israel Deaconess Medical Center, the chiefs of medicine, surgery, orthopedics, and other key functions presented Levy with special behavioral challenges, particularly because he was not a doctor. Each medical chief was in essence a "mini-dean," the head of a largely self-contained department with its own faculty, staff, and resources. As academic researchers, they were rewarded primarily for individual achievement. They had limited experience solving business or management problems.

In dealing with the chiefs, Levy chose an approach that blended with a strong dose of discipline with real-time, public reinforcement.

He developed guidelines for behavior and insisted that everyone in the hospital measure up to them. In one of his earliest meetings with the chiefs, Levy presented a simple set of "meeting rules," including such chestnuts as "state your objections" and "disagree without being disagreeable," and led a discussion about them, demonstrating the desired behaviors through his own leadership of the meeting. The purpose of these rules was to introduce new standards of interpersonal behavior and, in the process, to combat several dysfunctional routines.

One serious test of Levy's ability to reinforce these norms came a month and a half after he was named CEO. After a staff meeting at which all the department chairs were present, one chief—who had remained silent—sent an e-mail to Levy complaining about a decision made during the meeting. The e-mail copied the other chiefs as well as the chairman of the board. Many CEOs would choose to criticize such behavior privately. But Levy responded in an e-mail to the same audience, publicly denouncing the chief for his tone, his lack of civility, and his failure to speak up earlier in the process, as required by the new meeting rules. It was as close to a public hanging as anyone could get. Several of the chiefs privately expressed their support to Levy; they too had been offended by their peer's presumptuousness. More broadly, the open criticism served to powerfully reinforce new norms while curbing disruptive behavior.

Even as they must set expectations and reinforce behaviors, effective change leaders also recognize that many employees simply do not know how to make decisions as a group or work cooperatively. By delegating critical decisions and responsibilities, a leader can provide employees with ample opportunities to practice new ways of working; in such cases, employees' performance should be evaluated as much on their adherence to the new standards and processes as on their substantive choices. In this spirit, Levy chose to think of himself primarily as a kind of appeals court judge. When employees came to him seeking his intervention on an issue or situation, he explained, he would "review the process used by the 'lower court' to determine if it followed the rules. If so, the decision stands." He did not review cases de novo and substitute his judgment for that of the individual department or unit. He insisted that employees work through difficult issues themselves, even when they were not so inclined, rather than rely on him to tell them what to do. At other times, he intervened personally and coached employees when they lacked basic skills. When two members of his staff disagreed on a proposed course of action, Levy triggered an open, emotional debate, then worked with the participants and their bosses behind the scenes to resolve the differences. At the next staff meeting, he praised the participants' willingness to disagree publicly, reemphasizing that vigorous debate was healthy and desirable and that confrontation was not to be avoided. In this way, employees gained experience in working through their problems on their own.

Performance, of course, is the ultimate measure of a successful turnaround. On that score, BIDMC has done exceedingly well since Levy took the helm. The original restructuring plan called for a three-year improvement process, moving from a $58 million loss in 2001 to breakeven in 2004. At the end of the 2004 fiscal year, performance was far ahead of plan, with the hospital reporting a $37.4 million net gain from operations. Revenues were up, while costs were sharply reduced. Decision making was now crisper and more responsive, even though there was little change in the hospital's senior staff or medical leadership. Morale, not surprisingly, was up as well. To take just one indicator, annual nursing turnover, which was 15% to 16% when Levy became CEO, had dropped to 3% by mid-2004. Pleased with the hospital's performance, the board signed Levy to a new three-year contract.

Heads, Hearts, and Hands

It's clear that the key to Paul Levy's success at Beth Israel Deaconess Medical Center is that he understood the importance of making sure the cultural soil had been made ready before planting the seeds of change. In a receptive environment, employees not only understand why change is necessary; they're also emotionally committed to making it happen, and they faithfully execute the required steps.

On a cognitive level, employees in receptive environments are better able to let go of competing, unsubstantiated views of the nature and extent of the problems facing their organizations. They hold the same, objective views of the causes of poor performance. They acknowledge the seriousness of current financial, operational, and marketplace difficulties. And they take responsibility for their own contributions to those problems. Such a shared, fact-based diagnosis is crucial for moving forward.

On an emotional level, employees in receptive environments identify with the organization and its values and are committed to its continued existence. They believe that the organization stands for something more than profitability, market share, or stock performance and is therefore worth saving. Equally important, they trust the leader, believing that he or she shares their values and will fight to preserve them. Leaders earn considerable latitude from employees—and their proposals usually get the benefit of the doubt—when their hearts are thought to be in the right place.

Workers in such environments also have physical, hands-on experience with the new behaviors expected of them. They have seen the coming changes up close and understand what they are getting into. In such an atmosphere where it's acceptable for employees to wrestle with decisions on their own and practice unfamiliar ways of working, a leader can successfully allay irrational fears and undercut the myths that so often accompany major change efforts.

There is a powerful lesson in all this for leaders. To create a receptive environment, persuasion is the ultimate tool. Persuasion promotes understanding; understanding breeds acceptance; acceptance leads to action. Without persuasion, even the best of turnaround plans will fail to take root.

Originally published in February 2005. Reprint R0502F

Leading Change
When Business
Is Good

An Interview with *Samuel J. Palmisano.*
by Paul Hemp and Thomas A. Stewart

IN JULY 2003, *International Business Machines Corporation conducted a 72-hour experiment whose outcome was as uncertain as anything going on in its research labs. Six months into a top-to-bottom review of its management organization, IBM held a three-day discussion via the corporate intranet about the company's values. The forum, dubbed ValuesJam, joined thousands of employees in a debate about the very nature of the computer giant and what it stood for.*

Over the three days, an estimated 50,000 of IBM's employees— including CEO Sam Palmisano—checked out the discussion, posting nearly 10,000 comments about the proposed values. The jam had clearly struck a chord.

But it was a disturbingly dissonant one. Some comments were merely cynical. One had the subject line: "The only value in IBM today is the stock price." Another read, "Company values (ya right)." Others, though, addressed fundamental management issues. "I feel we talk a lot about trust and taking risks. But at the same time, we have endless audits, mistakes are punished and not seen as a welcome part of learning, and managers (and others) are consistently checked," wrote one employee. "There appears to be a great reluctance among our junior executive community to challenge the views of our senior execs," said another. "Many times I have heard expressions like, 'Would you tell Sam that his strategy is wrong!!?'" Twenty-four hours into the exercise, at least one senior executive wanted to pull the plug.

But Palmisano wouldn't hear of it. And then the mood began to shift. After a day marked by critics letting off steam, the countercritics began to weigh in. While acknowledging the company's shortcomings, they argued that much of IBM's culture and values was worth preserving. "Shortly after joining IBM 18 years ago," wrote one, "I was asked to serve on a jury. When I approached the bench and answered [the lawyers'] questions, I was surprised when the judge said, 'You guys can pick whoever else you want, but I want this IBMer on that jury.' I have never felt so much pride. His statement said it all: integrity, excellence, and quality." Comments like these became more frequent, criticism became more constructive, and the ValuesJam conversation stabilized.

The question of what was worth preserving and what needed to be changed was at the heart of ValuesJam. In 1914—when the company was making tabulating machines, scales for weighing meat, and cheese slicers—president Thomas Watson, Sr., decreed three corporate principles, called the Basic Beliefs: "respect for the individual," "the best customer service," and "the pursuit of excellence." They would inform IBM's culture, and help drive its success, for more than half a century.

By 2002, when Palmisano took over as CEO, much had happened to Big Blue. In the early 1990s, the company had suffered the worst reversal in its history and then, under Lou Gerstner, had fought its way back, transformed from a mainframe maker into a robust provider of integrated hardware, networking, and software solutions. Palmisano felt that the Basic Beliefs could still serve the company—but now as the foundation for a new set of corporate values that could energize employees even more than its near-death experience had. Looking for a modern-day equivalent, Palmisano first queried 300 of his senior executives, then quickly opened up the discussion, through a survey of over a thousand employees, to get a sense of how people at all levels, functions, and locations would articulate IBM's values and their

Idea in Brief

It's easy to fire up employees' passion for change when your business is about to go up in flames. Lou Gerstner knew this when he seized IBM's helm in 1993 and saved the faltering giant by transforming it from a mainframe maker into a provider of integrated solutions.

But how do you maintain people's commitment to change when business is *good*? *You* know your company must constantly adapt if it wants to maintain its competitive edge. Yet without an obvious threat on the horizon, your *employees* may grow complacent.

How to build a workforce of relentless change agents? Replace command-and-control with **values-based management**: Instead of galvanizing people through fear of failure, energize them through hope and aspiration. Inspire them to pursue a common purpose based on values *they* help to define. Ask them what's blocking them from living those values—and launch change initiatives to remove obstacles.

As enduring companies like IBM have discovered, values-based management enables your people to respond quickly, flexibly, and creatively to a never-ending stream of strategic challenges.

aspirations for the company. Out of this research grew the propositions that were debated in ValuesJam.

After—and even during—the jam, company analysts pored over the postings, mining the million-word text for key themes. Finally, a small team that included Palmisano came up with a revised set of corporate values. The CEO announced the new values to employees in an intranet broadcast in November 2003: "dedication to every client's success," "innovation that matters—for our company and for the world," "trust and personal responsibility in all relationships." Earthshaking? No, but imbued with legitimacy and packed with meaning and implications for IBM.

To prove that the new values were more than window dressing, Palmisano immediately made some changes. He called on the director of a major business unit—e-business hosting services for the U.S. industrial sector—and charged her with identifying gaps between the values and company practices. He bluntly told his 15 direct reports that they had better follow suit. Another online jam was held in Octo-

Idea in Practice

To create your values-based management system:

Gather Employees' Input on Values

Assess the strategic challenges facing your company. Propose values you believe will help your firm meet those challenges. Collect employees' feedback on your ideas.

> *Example:* IBM CEO Sam Palmisano knew that the IT industry was reintegrating: Customers wanted packages of computer products and services from single firms. Despite its far-flung, diverse 320,000-strong workforce, the company had to offer customized solutions at a single price. To achieve the required cooperation, IBM needed a shared set of values to guide people's decision making.

Using feedback from top managers and employees, Palmisano's team developed three working value statements—"Commitment to the customer," "Excellence through innovation," and "Integrity that earns trust." IBM posted these on its intranet and invited employees to debate them. Over three days, 50,000 debated the merits of the value statements.

Analyze Employees' Input

Examine employees' input for themes.

> *Example:* Many IBMers criticized the "integrity that earns trust" statement as vague, outdated, and inwardly focused. They wanted more specific guidance on how to behave with each other and with external stakeholders.

Revise Your Values

Based on the themes in employees' input, create a revised set of values. Gather employees' input again.

ber 2004 (this one informally dubbed a "logjam") in which employees were asked to identify organizational barriers to innovation and revenue growth.

Although Palmisano, by his own account, is building on a strategy laid down by Gerstner, the leadership styles of the two men are very different. Under Gerstner, there was little expansive talk about IBM's heritage. He was an outsider, a former CEO of RJR Nabisco and an ex-McKinsey consultant, who was faced with the daunting task of

Example: Palmisano's team revised the earlier value statements to read: "Dedication to every client's success," "Innovation that matters—for our company and for the world," and "Trust and personal responsibility in all relationships." The team published the revised statements on the intranet and once more invited feedback.

Identify Obstacles to Living the Values

Examine employees' responses to identify what's preventing your company from living its agreed-upon values.

Example: IBMers praised the revised value statements—often in highly emotional language—but wondered whether IBM was willing and able to live those values. They understood the need to

reintegrate the company but lamented obstacles—such as frustrating financial controls—that prevented them from serving customers quickly.

Launch Change Initiatives to Remove Obstacles

Initiate change programs that enable people to live the values.

Example: IBM allocated $5,000 a year to individual managers to use, no questions asked, in order to generate business, develop client relationships, or respond to fellow IBMers' emergency needs. A pilot program run with 700 client-facing teams showed that they spent the money intelligently. The program was expanded to all 22,000 IBM first-line managers. The initiative demonstrated to employees that IBM lives by its values.

righting a sinking ship. In fact, he famously observed, shortly after taking over, that "the last thing IBM needs right now is a vision." Palmisano, by contrast, is a true-blue IBMer, who started at the company in 1973 as a salesman in Baltimore. Like many of his generation who felt such acute shame when IBM was brought to its knees in the early 1990s, he clearly has a visceral attachment to the firm—and to the hope that it may someday regain its former greatness. At the same time, the erstwhile salesman is, in the words of a colleague, "a *results-driven, make-it-rain, close-the-deal sort of guy": not the first person you'd expect to hold forth on a subjective topic like "trust."*

In this edited conversation with HBR senior editor Paul Hemp and HBR's editor, Thomas A. Stewart, Palmisano talks about the strategic importance of values to IBM. He begins by explaining why—and how— hard financial metrics and soft corporate values can coexist.

Corporate values generally are feel-good statements that have almost no effect on a company's operations. What made—what makes—you think they can be more than this?

Look at the portrait of Tom Watson, Sr., in our lobby. You've never seen such a stern man. The eyes in the painting stare right through you. This was *not* a soft individual. He was a capitalist. He wanted IBM to make money, lots of it. But he was perceptive enough to build the company in a way that would ensure its prosperity long after he left the scene. His three Basic Beliefs successfully steered this company through persistent change and repeated reinvention for more than 50 years.

An organic system, which is what a company is, needs to adapt. And we think values—that's what we call them today at IBM, but you can call them "beliefs" or "principles" or "precepts" or even "DNA"— are what enable you to do that. They let you change everything, from your products to your strategies to your business model, but remain true to your essence, your basic mission and identity.

Unfortunately, over the decades, Watson's Basic Beliefs became distorted and took on a life of their own. "Respect for the individual" became entitlement: not fair work for all, not a chance to speak out, but a guaranteed job and culture-dictated promotions. "The pursuit of excellence" became arrogance: We stopped listening to our markets, to our customers, to each other. We were so successful for so long that we could never see another point of view. And when the market shifted, we almost went out of business. We had to cut a workforce of more than 400,000 people in half. Over the course of several years, we wiped out the equivalent of a medium-sized northeastern city—say, Providence, Rhode Island.

If you lived through this, as I did, it was easy to see how the company's values had become part of the problem. But I believe values can once again help guide us through major change and meet some of the formidable challenges we face.

For instance, I feel that a strong value system is crucial to bringing together and motivating a workforce as large and diverse as ours has become. We have nearly one-third of a million employees serving clients in 170 countries. Forty percent of those people don't report daily to an IBM site; they work on the client's premises, from home, or they're mobile. And, perhaps most significant, given IBM's tradition of hiring and training young people for a lifetime of work, half of today's employees have been with the company for fewer than five years because of recent acquisitions and our relatively new practice of hiring seasoned professionals. In a modest hiring year, we now add 20,000 to 25,000 people.

In effect, gradually repopulating Providence, Rhode Island!

Exactly. So how do you channel this diverse and constantly changing array of talent and experience into a common purpose? How do you get people to *passionately* pursue that purpose?

You could employ all kinds of traditional, top-down management processes. But they wouldn't work at IBM—or, I would argue, at an increasing number of twenty-first-century companies. You just can't impose command-and-control mechanisms on a large, highly professional workforce. I'm not only talking about our scientists, engineers, and consultants. More than 200,000 of our employees have college degrees. The CEO can't say to them, "Get in line and follow me." Or "*I've* decided what *your* values are." They're too smart for that. And as you know, smarter people tend to be, well, a little more challenging; you might even say cynical.

But even if our people did accept this kind of traditional, hierarchical management system, our clients wouldn't. As we learned at IBM over the years, a top-down system can create a smothering bureaucracy that doesn't allow for the speed, the flexibility, the innovation that clients expect today.

So you're saying that values are about how employees behave when management isn't there, which it can't be—which it shouldn't be—given IBM's size and the need for people to make decisions quickly. You're basically talking about using values to manage.

Yes. A values-based management system. Let me cast the issue in a slightly different light. When you think about it, there's no optimal way to organize IBM. We traditionally were viewed as a large, successful, "well-managed" company. That was a compliment. But in today's fast-changing environment, it's a problem. You can easily end up with a bureaucracy of people overanalyzing problems and slowing down the decision-making process.

Think of our organizational matrix. Remember, we operate in 170 countries. To keep it simple, let's say we have 60 or 70 major product lines. We have more than a dozen customer segments. Well, if you mapped out the entire 3-D matrix, you'd get more than 100,000 cells—cells in which you have to close out P&Ls every day, make decisions, allocate resources, make trade-offs. You'll drive people crazy trying to centrally manage every one of those intersections.

So if there's no way to optimize IBM through organizational structure or by management dictate, you have to empower people while ensuring that they're making the right calls the right way. And by "right," I'm not talking about ethics and legal compliance alone; those are table stakes. I'm talking about decisions that support and give life to IBM's strategy and brand, decisions that shape a culture. That's why values, for us, aren't soft. They're the basis of what we do, our mission as a company. They're a touchstone for decentralized decision making. It used to be a rule of thumb that "people don't do what you expect; they do what you inspect." My point is that it's just not possible to inspect everyone anymore. But you also can't just let go of the reins and let people do what they want without guidance or context. You've got to create a management system that empowers people and provides a basis for decision making that is consistent with who we are at IBM.

How do the new values help further IBM's strategy?

In two main ways. Back some 12 years ago, three-fifths of our business was in computer hardware and roughly two-fifths was in software and services. Today, those numbers are more than reversed. Well, if three-fifths of your business is manufacturing, management is basically supervisory: "You do this. You do that." But that no longer works when your business is primarily based on knowledge. And your business model also changes dramatically.

For one thing, people—rather than products—become your brand. Just as our products have had to be consistent with the IBM brand promise, now more than ever, so do our people. One way to ensure that is to inform their behavior with a globally consistent set of values.

Second, the IT industry has continued to shift toward reintegration. We all know the story of how the industry fragmented in the 1980s and 1990s, with separate companies selling the processors, the storage devices, and the software that make up a computer system—almost killing IBM, the original vertically integrated computer company. Now customers are demanding a package of computer products and services from a single company, a company that can offer them an integrated solution to their business problems. This is a big opportunity for IBM. We probably have a wider array of computer products and services and know-how than anyone. But it's also a challenge. How can we get our people in far-flung business units with different financial targets and incentives working together in teams that can offer at a single price a comprehensive and customized solution—one that doesn't show the organizational seams?

Companies usually face the issue of workforce integration after a huge merger. We needed to integrate our existing workforce as a strategic response to the reintegration of the industry. It won't surprise you that I didn't think the answer lay in a new organizational structure or in more management oversight. What you need to foster this sort of cooperation is a common set of guidelines about how we make decisions, day in and day out. In other words, values.

And what happens when the strategy changes?

Ah, that's why the right set of values is so important. There's always going to be another strategy on the horizon as the market changes, as technologies come and go. So we wanted values that would foster an organization able to quickly execute a new strategy. At the same time, we wanted values that, like Watson's Basic Beliefs, would be enduring, that would guide the company through economic cycles and geopolitical shifts, that would transcend changes in products, technologies, employees, and leaders.

How did IBM distill new values from its past traditions and current employee feedback?

The last time IBM examined its values was nearly a century ago. Watson was an entrepreneur, leading what was, in today's lingo, a start-up. So in 1914, he simply said, "Here are our beliefs. Learn them. Live them." That was appropriate for his day, and there's no question it worked. But 90 years later, we couldn't have someone in headquarters sitting up in bed in the middle of the night and saying, "Here are our new values!" We couldn't be casual about tinkering with the DNA of a company like IBM. We had to come up with a way to get the employees to create the value system, to determine the company's principles. Watson's Basic Beliefs, however distorted they might have become over the years, had to be the starting point.

After getting input from IBM's top 300 executives and conducting focus groups with more than a thousand employees—a statistically representative cross-section—we came up with three perfectly sound values. [For a detailed description of how IBM got from the Basic Beliefs to its new set of values, see the sidebar "Continuity and Change."] But I knew we'd eventually throw out the statements to everyone in the company to debate. That's where ValuesJam came in—this live, companywide conversation on our intranet.

What was your own experience during the jam? Did you have the feeling you'd opened Pandora's box?

I logged in from China. I was pretty jet-lagged and couldn't sleep, so I jumped in with postings on a lot of stuff, particularly around client issues. [For a selection of Palmisano's postings during the Values-Jam, see the sidebar "Sam Joins the Fray."] And yes, the electronic argument was hot and contentious and messy. But you had to get comfortable with that. Understand, we had done three or four big online jams before this, so we had some idea of how lively they can be. Even so, none of those could have prepared us for the emotions unleashed by this topic.

You had to put your ego aside—not easy for a CEO to do—and realize that this was the best thing that could have happened. You could say, "Oh my God, I've unleashed this incredible negative energy." Or you could say, "Oh my God, I now have this incredible mandate to drive even more change in the company."

When Lou Gerstner came here in 1993, there was clearly a burning platform. In fact, the whole place was in flames. There was even talk of breaking up the company. And he responded brilliantly. Here's this outsider who managed to marshal the collective urgency of tens of thousands of people like me to save this company and turn it around: without a doubt one of the greatest saves in business history. But the trick then wasn't creating a sense of urgency—we had that. Maybe you needed to shake people out of being shell-shocked. But most IBMers were willing to do whatever it took to save the company, not to mention their own jobs. And there was a lot of pride at stake. Lou's task was mostly to convince people that he was making the right changes.

Once things got better, though, there was another kind of danger: that we would slip back into complacency. As our financial results improved dramatically and we began outperforming our competitors, people—already weary from nearly a decade of change—would say, "Well, why do I have to do things differently now? The leadership may be different, but the strategy is fundamentally sound. Why do I have to change?" This is, by the way, a problem that everyone running a successful company wrestles with.

So the challenge shifted. Instead of galvanizing people through fear of failure, you have to galvanize them through hope and aspiration. You lay out the opportunity to become a great company again—the greatest in the world, which is what IBM used to be. And you hope people feel the same need, the urgency you do, to get there. Well, I think IBMers today do feel that urgency. Maybe the jam's greatest contribution was to make that fact unambiguously clear to all of us, very visibly, in public.

Continuity and Change

IBM'S NEW VALUES GREW OUT OF A LONG TRADITION. In 1914, Thomas Watson, Sr., the founder of the modern International Business Machines Corporation, laid out three principles known as the *Basic Beliefs*:

- Respect for the individual
- The best customer service
- The pursuit of excellence

Although these beliefs played a significant role in driving IBM's success over most of the twentieth century, they eventually were subsumed—and, in effect, redefined—by a sense of entitlement and arrogance within the organization. That, according to CEO Sam Palmisano, contributed to the company's failure to respond to market changes in the early 1990s and to its near demise.

In February 2003, just under a year after taking over as CEO, at a meeting of IBM's top 300 managers, Palmisano raised the idea of reinventing the company's values as a way to manage and reintegrate the sprawling and diverse enterprise. He put forth *four concepts*, three of them drawn from Watson's Basic Beliefs, as possible bases for the new values:

- Respect
- Customer
- Excellence
- Innovation

These were "test marketed" through surveys and focus groups with more than 1,000 IBM employees. The notion of "respect" was thrown out because of its connotations of the past. It was also decided that statements rather than just words would be more compelling.

Out of this process grew the three *proposed values* discussed during the July 2003 online forum, ValuesJam:

- Commitment to the customer

What were the chief points of debate—or contention?

There was actually remarkable agreement on *what* we all value. The debate, as it turned out, wasn't over the values themselves so much. The debate was about whether IBM today is willing and able to live them.

For instance, people seemed to understand the need to reintegrate the company, but there were complaints—legitimate complaints—

- Excellence through innovation
- Integrity that earns trust

Using a specially tailored "jamalyzer" tool—based on IBM's e-classifier software, but turbocharged with additional capabilities designed to process constantly changing content—IBM analysts crunched the million-plus words posted during the ValuesJam. Some themes emerged. For example, many people said that a silo mentality pitted the business units against one another, to the detriment of IBM as a whole. Several people characterized this as a trust issue. But the proposed value "integrity that earns trust" was criticized as being too vague. Some thought it was just another way of saying "respect for the individual," one of the original Basic Beliefs that many now viewed as outdated. And the notion of trust was seen as being too inwardly focused—management trusting its employees—and not prescriptive enough in terms of how employees should behave with each other or with parties outside the company.

Drawing on this analysis, the results of pre- and post-jam surveys, and a full reading of the raw transcripts, a small team, with input from Palmisano, arrived at a revised set of *new corporate values*:

- **Dedication to every client's success**
- **Innovation that matters—for our company and for the world**
- **Trust and personal responsibility in all relationships**

These were published on the company intranet in November 2003.

about things that are getting in the way. People would describe extremely frustrating situations. They'd say something like: "I'm in Tokyo, prototyping software for a client, and I need a software engineer based in Austin *right now* to help in a blade server configuration. But I can't just say, 'Please come to Tokyo and help.' I need to get a charge code first so I can pay his department for his time!"

There's a collective impatience that we've been tapping into to drive the change needed to make IBM everything that all of us aspire for it to be. I'm convinced that we wouldn't have gotten to this point if we hadn't found a way to engage the entire IBM population in a genuine, candid conversation.

Sam Joins the Fray

IBM CEO SAM PALMISANO was in China on business during ValuesJam, and he logged on from there. Following are some of his comments (typos included) on a number of topics raised by employees during the online forum:

YES, values matter!!!!! (6 reply)

Samuel J. Palmisano 29 Jul 2003 20:00 GMT

Good discussion about the need for values/principles/belifes, etc. people can be very cynical and sarcastic about this kind of topic,but I appreciate the thoughtful constructive comments I'm seeing. Personaly, I believe "values" should embrace a company's broader role in the world —with customers, society, culture,etc. - as well as how its people work together.. I hope this Jam elevates IBMs ambitions about its mission inthe 21st century.. WE have a unique opprtunity for IBM to set the pace for ALL companies, not just the techs.

doing the right thing for customers . . . (21 reply)

Samuel J. Palmisano 29 Jul 2003 20:07 GMT

Early in my career when I was in the field in Baltimore,one of our systems failed for a healthcare customer. The customer went to manual processes,but said they would start losing patients within hours if the system couldnt be fixed. The branch mgr called one of our competitors and orderd another system. so two teams of IBMERS worked side by side.. one to fix the system, the others to bring up the new one. the mgr never asked Hq what to do.. it was a great lesson in how far this company will go to help a customer in time of need. btw, we fixed the system in time.

By the way, having a global, universally accessible intranet like ours certainly helps, but the technology isn't the point. I think we would've found a way to have this companywide dialogue if the Web didn't exist. [For an explanation of how the jam worked, see the sidebar "Managing ValuesJam."]

What happened after the jam?

Well, we got a mountain of employee comments. The team analyzed all of it, and it was clear that the proposed value statements needed to change to reflect some of the nuances and emotion people expressed. So, drawing on this analysis, along with other employee feedback, a small team settled on IBM's new corporate values.

integrity/trust in ALL our relationships matter!!!! (44 reply)

Samuel J. Palmisano 29 Jul 2003 20:12 GMT

very interesting discussion . . . one thing I'm noticing, and it was in the broadcast feedback too: not too many of you are talking about integrity and trust when it comes to our OTHER relationships that are key to IBMs success—customers, communities where we live, owners of the company etc. any thoghts on why thats so? maybe we're too inwardly focused?

a world without IBM???? (35 reply)

Samuel J. Palmisano 29 Jul 2003 20:20 GMT

No IBM? the industry would stop growing because no one would invent anything that ran for more than THREE MINUTES.. no IBM means no grownups . . . no IBM means no truly global company that brings economic growth, respect progress to societies everywhere . . . no iBM means no place to work for hundreds of thousands of people who want more than a job, they want to ,MAKE A DIFFERENCE in the world.

suggestion for Sam (9 reply)

Samuel J. Palmisano 29 Jul 2003 20:25 GMT

steve, you make good points about how/when we win . . . we can blow up more burecracy if we all behave like mature adutls and take into account ALL OF THE INTERESTS of IBm FIRST.. customers, employees, shareholders, doing whats right for the LONG TERM intersts of the company. mgrs have an importrant role to play in encouraing this kind of behavior . . . you have my support.

The first value is "dedication to every client's success." At one level, that's pretty straightforward: Bring together all of IBM's capability—in the laboratory, in the field, in the back office, wherever—to help solve difficult problems clients can't solve themselves. But this is also a lot more than the familiar claim of unstinting customer service. "Client success" isn't just "the customer is always right." It means maintaining a long-term relationship where what happens after the deal is more important than what happens before it's signed. It means a persistent focus on outcomes. It means having skin in the game of your client's success, up to and including how your contracts are structured and what triggers your getting paid.

The second is "innovation that matters—for our company and for the world." When employees talked about IBM making a difference in the world, they included more than our work of inventing and building great products. They talked about how their work touches people and society, how we can help save lives—say, through our cutting-edge work with the Mayo Clinic or by helping governments fight terrorism with our data technology. This kind of innovation is a major reason we are able to attract great scientists. They can do cool stuff and maybe make more money in Silicon Valley—for a while, anyway—but they can do work that actually changes business and society at IBM. And it's also about what I mentioned before: a continually experimental attitude toward IBM itself. Over most of our 90 years, with the exception of that one period when we became arrogant and complacent, this company never stopped questioning assumptions, trying out different models, testing the limits—whether in technology or business or in progressive workforce policies. Employees reminded us that those things are innovations that matter at least as much as new products.

The third value is "trust and personal responsibility in all relationships." There's a lot in that statement, too. Interestingly, the feedback from employees on this value has focused on relationships among people at IBM. But we're also talking about the company's relationships with suppliers, with investors, with governments, with communities.

We published the values in their final form—along with some elaboration on them and some direct employee postings from the jam—in November 2003. Over the next ten days, more than 200,000 people downloaded the online document. The responses just flooded in, both in the form of postings on the intranet and in more than a thousand e-mails sent directly to me, telling us in often sharp language just where IBM's operations fell short of, or clashed with, these ideals. Some of the comments were painful to read. But, again, they exhibited something every leader should welcome: People here aren't complacent about the company's future. And the comments were, by and large, extremely thoughtful.

Managing ValuesJam

IBM HAD EXPERIMENTED before with jam sessions—relatively unstructured employee discussions around broad topics—both on the corporate intranet and in face-to-face off-site brainstorming sessions. But the 72-hour Values-Jam, held in July 2003, was the most ambitious, focusing as it did on the very nature and future of IBM.

One thing was clear: You wouldn't be able to orchestrate a forum like this, the verbal equivalent of an improvisational jam session among jazz musicians. In the words of CEO Sam Palmisano, "It just took off." But, much like a musical jam, the dialogue was informed by a number of themes:

Forum 1. Company Values

Do company values exist? If so, what is involved in establishing them? Most companies today have values statements. But what would a company look and act like that truly lived its beliefs? Is it important for IBM to agree on a set of lasting values that drive everything it does?

Forum 2. A First Draft

What values are essential to what IBM needs to become? Consider this list: 1. Commitment to the customer. 2. Excellence through innovation. 3. Integrity that earns trust. How might these values change the way we act or the decisions we make? Is there some important aspect or nuance that is missing?

Forum 3. A Company's Impact

If our company disappeared tonight, how different would the world be tomorrow? Is there something about our company that makes a unique contribution to the world?

Forum 4. The Gold Standard

When is IBM at its best? When have you been proudest to be an IBMer? What happened, and what was uniquely meaningful about it? And what do we need to do—or change—to be the gold standard going forward?

What did you do with this feedback?

We collected and collated it. Then I printed all of it out—the stack of paper was about three feet high—and took it home to read over one weekend. On Monday morning, I walked into our executive committee meeting and threw it on the table. I said, "You guys ought to read every one of these comments, because if you think we've got this place plumbed correctly, think again."

Don't get me wrong. The passion in these e-mails was positive as well as negative. People would say, literally, "I'm weeping. These values describe the company I joined, the company I believe in. We can truly make this place great again. But we've got all these things in our way. . . ." The raw emotion of some of the e-mails was really something.

Now, if you've unleashed all this frustration and energy, if you've invited people to feel hope about something they really care about, you'd better be prepared to do something in response. So, in the months since we finalized the values, we've announced some initiatives that begin to close the gaps.

One I have dubbed our "$100 million bet on trust." We kept hearing about situations like our colleague in Tokyo who needed help from the engineer in Austin, cases in which employees were unable to respond quickly to client needs because of financial control processes that required several levels of management approval. The money would usually be approved, but too late. So we allocated managers up to $5,000 annually they could spend, no questions asked, to respond to extraordinary situations that would help generate business or develop client relationships or to respond to an IBMer's emergency need. We ran a pilot for a few months with our 700 client-facing teams, and they spent the money intelligently. There were lots of examples of teams winning deals and delighting clients with a small amount of "walk around money" to spend at their discretion. So, based on the success of that pilot, we expanded the program to all 22,000 IBM first-line managers.

You can do the math: $5,000 times 22,000 managers is a big number. I'm sure there were people in the company who said, "We need to get this under control." But they're not the CEO. Yes, you need financial controls. Yes, not every dollar spent from this Managers' Value Fund will yield some tangible return. But I'm confident that allowing line managers to take some reasonable risks, and trusting them with those decisions, will pay off over time. The program also makes a point: that we live by our values.

The value of "trust and personal responsibility in all relationships"—including those with IBM's shareholders—led to another initiative: a change in the way we grant top executive stock options. After getting a lot of outside experts to study this (and concluding that the complicated algorithms they recommended were wonderful, if you wanted to hire the outsiders as permanent consultants, but terrible if you wanted a simple formula that aligned executive behavior with shareholder interests), we settled on a straightforward idea. Senior executives will benefit from their options only after shareholders have realized at least 10% growth in their investments—that is, the strike price is 10% higher than the market price on the day the options are issued. Look at it this way: IBM's market value would have to increase by $17 billion from that date before any of the execs realize a penny of benefit. We think we are the first large company to take such a radical step—and it grew out of our values.

Let me give you one more example. It may not sound like a big deal, but for us, it was radical. We overhauled the way we set prices. We heard time and again from employees about how difficult it was to put together a client-friendly, cross-IBM solution, one involving a variety of products and services at a single, all-inclusive price. We couldn't do it. Every brand unit had its own P&L, and all the people who determine prices had been organized by brand. Remember those 100,000 cells in our 3-D matrix? Our people were pulling their cross-IBM bids apart, running them through our financial-accounting system as separate bids for individual products and services. This was nuts, because it's our ability to offer everything—hardware, software, services, and financing—that gives us a real advantage. When we bid on each of the parts separately, we go head-to-head against rivals by product: EMC in storage, say, or Accenture in services. This was tearing out the very heart of our strategy of integration, not to mention our unique kind of business-plus-technology innovation.

Let me give you a humorous (if somewhat discouraging) illustration. Every senior executive has responsibility for at least one major client—we call them "partnership accounts." Our former CFO John Joyce, who now heads IBM's services business, put together a deal for his account that involved some hardware, some software, and some services. He was told he couldn't price it as an integrated solution. And he's the CFO! So we figured out a way to set a single price for each integrated offering.

This sounds like a great business move. But what does it have to do with values? Wouldn't you ultimately have decided you had to do that in any case?

To be honest, we'd been debating the pricing issue at the executive level for a long time. But we hadn't done anything about it. The values initiative forced us to confront the issue, and it gave us the impetus to make the change. You know, there are always ingrained operations and habits of mind in any organization—I don't care whether it's a business or a university or a government. Well, the values and the jam were great inertia-busting vehicles. A small business in this place is $15 billion, and a big one is $40 billion. So you have senior vice presidents running Fortune 500–sized companies who aren't necessarily looking for bright ideas from the CEO or some task force every day. But when you hear from so many of our people on the front lines, you can't just ignore it. They're crying out: "We say we value 'client success,' and we want to grow our business. This one thing is getting in the way of both!" You've got to pay attention—if not to me, then to them.

So we took the pricers—the people who set the prices for client bids—and we said to them, "You work for IBM. When there's a cross-IBM bid with multiple products, you price it on the IBM income statement, not on the income statements of each product." Needless to say, this involved a series of very difficult meetings with senior executives. There was a huge debate among the finance people about all the reasons why we couldn't do it: "It will be too much work to reallocate all the costs and revenue of a project back to individual profit centers." And they're right: It isn't easy, especially when we now have to certify everything. But the CFO was with me on this: After all, he'd seen the problem firsthand! And we made the change, so that now when we make a truly cross-IBM bid, we can optimize it for the client and for us.

This brings us back to the tension between soft values and hard financial metrics. In the long run, they shouldn't conflict. But along the way, they're going to be jabbing at each other. After all, people still have to make their numbers.

Certainly, there's no getting around that in a commercial enterprise. But I think values inject balance in the company's culture and management system: balance between the short-term transaction and the long-term relationship, balance between the interests of shareholders, employees, and clients. In every case, you have to make a call. Values help you make those decisions, not on an ad hoc basis, but in a way that is consistent with your culture and brand, with who you are as a company.

Look at how we compensate our managing directors, who are responsible for our largest client relationships. We decided to take half their comp and calculate it not on an annual basis but on a rolling three-year basis. We ask clients to score the managing director's performance at the end of a project or engagement, which might last longer than a single year, and that plays a big part in his bonus. So a big piece of his compensation is based on a combination of the project's profitability—whether the manager made his annual numbers—and on the client's satisfaction over a longer-term horizon. The managing director can't trade off one for the other.

So we've tried to keep balance in the system, to make sure that things aren't completely oriented toward short-term financials. But you're absolutely right: There are times when people will argue, "Well, jeez, you guys are pushing us in both directions." It's a valid debate. I think, though, that the best place to have that debate is at the lowest level of your organization, because that's where these decisions are being made and having an impact. Thousands of these interactions go on every day that none of us at the top will ever, or should ever, know about. But you hope that the values are providing a counterweight to the drive for short-term profitability in all those interactions. In the long term, I think, whether or not you have a values-driven culture is what makes you a winner or a loser.

You've had the new values in place for just about a year now.
They've already created strong emotions and high expectations.
What's the prognosis?

We're just starting down the road on what is probably a ten- to 15-year process. I was back in Asia not long ago, and I did one of these town hall–style meetings with IBM employees and talked about the values. Probably two-thirds of the people clearly knew about them, had read about them. But a third of the people—you could look at their faces and see it—hadn't even heard of the values. Or at least the values hadn't resonated with them yet. So we have work to do. Not just in getting everyone to memorize three pithy statements. We need to do a heck of a lot to close the gaps between our stated values and the reality of IBM today. That's the point of it all.

I know that not everyone on my executive team is as enthusiastic about the values initiative as I am—though they'd never admit it! But people on the senior team who lived through IBM's near-death experience will do anything not to go back to that. The blow to everyone's pride when IBM became the laughingstock of the business world was almost too much to bear. I have zero resistance from the senior team to initiatives that can save us from a return to that. And our values work is one of the most important of those initiatives.

Then look at the employee response to ValuesJam. There is an unmistakable yearning for this to be a great company. I mean, why have people joined IBM over the years? There are a lot of places to make money, if that's what drives you. Why come here?

I believe it's because they want to be part of a progressive company that makes a difference in the world. They want to be in the kind of company that supports research that wins Nobel Prizes, that changes the way people think about business itself, that is willing to take firm positions on unpopular issues based on principle.

You know, back in the 1950s, Watson, Jr., wrote the governors of southern states that IBM would not adhere to separate-but-equal laws, and then the company codified an equal-opportunity policy years before it was mandated by law. I've got to believe that a company that conceives of itself that way, and that seriously manages itself accordingly, has strong appeal to a lot of people. We can't offer them the promise of instant wealth, which they may get at a start-up, or a job for life, as in the old days. But we can offer them something worth believing in and working toward.

If we get most people in this company excited about that, they're going to pull the rest of the company with them. If they become dedicated to these values and what we're trying to accomplish, I can go to sleep at night confident of our future.

Originally published in December 2004. Reprint R0412C

Radical Change, the Quiet Way

by Debra E. Meyerson

AT ONE POINT OR ANOTHER, many managers experience a spang of conscience—a yearning to confront the basic or hidden assumptions, interests, practices, or values within an organization that they feel are stodgy, unfair, even downright wrong. A vice president wishes that more people of color would be promoted. A partner at a consulting firm thinks new MBAs are being so overworked that their families are hurting. A senior manager suspects his company, with some extra cost, could be kinder to the environment. Yet many people who want to drive changes like these face an uncomfortable dilemma. If they speak out too loudly, resentment builds toward them; if they play by the rules and remain silent, resentment builds inside them. Is there any way, then, to rock the boat without falling out of it?

Over the past 15 years, I have studied hundreds of professionals who spend the better part of their work lives trying to answer this question. Each one of the people I've studied differs from the organizational status quo in some way—in values, race, gender, or sexual preference, perhaps (see the sidebar "How the Research Was Done"). They all see things a bit differently from the "norm." But despite feeling at odds with aspects of the prevailing culture, they genuinely like their jobs and want to continue to succeed in them, to effectively use their differences as the impetus for constructive change.

How the Research Was Done

THIS ARTICLE IS BASED ON a multipart research effort that I began in 1986 with Maureen Scully, a professor of management at the Center for Gender in Organizations at Simmons Graduate School of Management in Boston. We had observed a number of people in our own occupation—academia—who, for various reasons, felt at odds with the prevailing culture of their institutions. Initially, we set out to understand how these individuals sustained their sense of self amid pressure to conform and how they managed to uphold their values without jeopardizing their careers. Eventually, this research broadened to include interviews with individuals in a variety of organizations and occupations: business people, doctors, nurses, lawyers, architects, administrators, and engineers at various levels of seniority in their organizations.

Since 1986, I have observed and interviewed dozens of tempered radicals in many occupations and conducted focused research with 236 men and women, ranging from mid-level professionals to CEOs. The sample was diverse, including people of different races, nationalities, ages, religions, and sexual orientations, and people who hold a wide range of values and change agendas. Most of these people worked in one of three publicly traded corporations—a financial services organization, a high-growth computer components corporation, and a company that makes and sells consumer products. In this portion of the research, I set out to learn more about the challenges tempered radicals face and discover their strategies for surviving, thriving, and fomenting change. The sum of this research resulted in the spectrum of strategies described in this article.

They believe that direct, angry confrontation will get them nowhere, but they don't sit by and allow frustration to fester. Rather, they work quietly to challenge prevailing wisdom and gently provoke their organizational cultures to adapt. I call such change agents *tempered radicals* because they work to effect significant changes in moderate ways.

In so doing, they exercise a form of leadership within organizations that is more localized, more diffuse, more modest, and less visible than traditional forms—yet no less significant. In fact, top executives seeking to institute cultural or organizational change—who are, perhaps, moving tradition-bound organizations down new roads or who are concerned about reaping the full potential of marginalized employees—might do well to seek out these tempered

Idea in Brief

How do you rock your corporate boat—without falling out? You know your firm needs constructive change, but here's your dilemma: If you push your agenda too hard, resentment builds against you. If you remain silent, resentment builds inside you.

What's a manager to do? Become a **tempered radical**—an informal leader who quietly challenges prevailing wisdom and provokes cultural transformation. These radicals bear no banners and sound no trumpets. Their seemingly innocuous changes barely inspire notice. But like steady drops of water, they gradually erode granite.

Tempered radicals embody contrasts. Their commitments are firm, but their means flexible. They yearn for rapid change, but trust in patience. They often work alone, yet unite others. Rather than pressing their agendas, they start conversations. And instead of battling powerful foes, they seek powerful friends. The over-all effect? Evolutionary—but relentless—change.

radicals, who may be hidden deep within their own organizations. Because such individuals are both dedicated to their companies and masters at changing organizations at the grassroots level, they can prove extremely valuable in helping top managers to identify fundamental causes of discord, recognize alternative perspectives, and adapt to changing needs and circumstances. In addition, tempered radicals, given support from above and a modicum of room to experiment, can prove to be excellent leaders. (For more on management's role in fostering tempered radicals, see the sidebar "Tempered Radicals as Everyday Leaders.")

Since the actions of tempered radicals are not, by design, dramatic, their leadership may be difficult to recognize. How, then, do people who run organizations, who want to nurture this diffuse source of cultural adaptation, find and develop these latent leaders? One way is to appreciate the variety of modes in which tempered radicals operate, learn from them, and support their efforts.

To navigate between their personal beliefs and the surrounding cultures, tempered radicals draw principally on a spectrum of incremental approaches, including four I describe here. I call these *disruptive self-expression, verbal jujitsu, variable-term opportunism,*

Idea in Practice

Tempered radicals use these tactics:

Disruptive Self-Expression

Demonstrate your values through your language, dress, office décor, or behavior. People notice and talk— often becoming brave enough to try the change themselves. The more people talk, the greater the impact.

Example: Stressed-out manager John Ziwak began arriving at work earlier so he could leave by 6:00 p.m. to be with family. He also refused evening business calls. As his stress eased, his performance improved. Initially skeptical, colleagues soon accommodated, finding more efficient ways of working and achieving balance in their own lives.

Verbal Jujitsu

Redirect negative statements or actions into positive change.

Example: Sales manager Brad Williams noticed that the new marketing director's peers ignored her during meetings. When one of them co-opted a thought she had already expressed, Williams said: "I'm glad George picked up on Sue's concerns. Sue, did George correctly capture what you were thinking?" No one ignored Sue again.

Variable-Term Opportunism

Be ready to capitalize on unexpected opportunities for short-term change, as well as orchestrate deliberate, longer term change.

and *strategic alliance building*. Disruptive self-expression, in which an individual simply acts in a way that feels personally right but that others notice, is the most inconspicuous way to initiate change. Verbal jujitsu turns an insensitive statement, action, or behavior back on itself. Variable-term opportunists spot, create, and capitalize on short- and long-term opportunities for change. And with the help of strategic alliances, an individual can push through change with more force.

Each of these approaches can be used in many ways, with plenty of room for creativity and wit. Self-expression can be done with a whisper; an employee who seeks more racial diversity in the ranks might wear her dashiki to company parties. Or it can be done with a roar; that same employee might wear her dashiki to the office every day. Similarly, a person seeking stricter environmental policies

Example: Senior executive Jane Adams joined a company with a dog-eat-dog culture. To insinuate her collaborative style, she shared power with direct reports, encouraged them to also delegate, praised them publicly, and invited them to give high-visibility presentations. Her division gained repute as an exceptional training ground for building experience, responsibility, and confidence.

Strategic Alliance Building

Gain clout by working with allies. Enhance your legitimacy and implement change more quickly and directly than you could alone. Don't make "opponents" enemies—they're often your best source of support and resources.

Example: Paul Wielgus started a revolution in his bureaucratic global spirits company—by persuading the opposition to join him. Others derided the training department Wielgus formed to boost employee creativity, and an auditor scrutinized the department for unnecessary expense. Rather than getting defensive, Paul treated the auditor as an equal and sold him on the program's value. The training spread, inspiring employees and enhancing productivity throughout the company.

might build an alliance by enlisting the help of one person, the more powerful the better. Or he might post his stance on the company intranet and actively seek a host of supporters. Taken together, the approaches form a continuum of choices from which tempered radicals draw at different times and in various circumstances.

But before looking at the approaches in detail, it's worth reconsidering, for a moment, the ways in which cultural change happens in the workplace.

How Organizations Change

Research has shown that organizations change primarily in two ways: through drastic action and through evolutionary adaptation. In the former case, change is discontinuous and often forced on the

Tempered Radicals as Everyday Leaders

IN THE COURSE OF THEIR DAILY actions and interactions, tempered radicals teach important lessons and inspire change. In so doing, they exercise a form of leadership within organizations that is less visible than traditional forms—but just as important.

The trick for organizations is to locate and nurture this subtle form of leadership. Consider how Barry Coswell, a conservative, yet open-minded lawyer who headed up the securities division of a large, distinguished financial services firm, identified, protected, and promoted a tempered radical within his organization. Dana, a left-of-center, first-year attorney, came to his office on her first day of work after having been fingerprinted—a standard practice in the securities industry. The procedure had made Dana nervous: What would happen when her new employer discovered that she had done jail time for participating in a 1960s-era civil rights protest? Dana quickly understood that her only hope of survival was to be honest about her background and principles. Despite the difference in their political proclivities, she decided to give Barry the benefit of the doubt. She marched into his office and confessed to having gone to jail for sitting in front of a bus.

"I appreciate your honesty," Barry laughed, "but unless you've broken a securities law, you're probably okay." In return for her small confidence, Barry shared stories of his own about growing up in a poor county and about his life in the military. The story swapping allowed them to put aside ideological disagreements and to develop a deep respect for each other. Barry sensed a

organization or mandated by top management in the wake of major technological innovations, by a scarcity or abundance of critical resources, or by sudden changes in the regulatory, legal, competitive, or political landscape. Under such circumstances, change may happen quickly and often involves significant pain. Evolutionary change, by contrast, is gentle, incremental, decentralized, and over time produces a broad and lasting shift with less upheaval.

The power of evolutionary approaches to promote cultural change is the subject of frequent discussion. For instance, in "We Don't Need Another Hero" (HBR, September 2001), Joseph L. Badaracco, Jr., asserts that the most effective moral leaders often operate beneath the radar, achieving their reforms without widespread notice. Likewise, tempered radicals gently and continually budding leader in Dana. Here was a woman who operated on the strength of her convictions and was honest about it but was capable of discussing her beliefs without self-righteousness. She didn't pound tables. She was a good conversationalist. She listened attentively. And she was able to elicit surprising confessions from him.

Barry began to accord Dana a level of protection, and he encouraged her to speak her mind, take risks, and most important, challenge his assumptions. In one instance, Dana spoke up to defend a female junior lawyer who was being evaluated harshly and, Dana believed, inequitably. Dana observed that different standards were being applied to male and female lawyers, but her colleagues dismissed her "liberal" concerns. Barry cast a glance at Dana, then said to the staff, "Let's look at this and see if we are being too quick to judge." After the meeting, Barry and Dana held a conversation about double standards and the pervasiveness of bias. In time, Barry initiated a policy to seek out minority legal counsel, both in-house and at outside legal firms. And Dana became a senior vice president.

In Barry's ability to recognize, mentor, and promote Dana there is a key lesson for executives who are anxious to foster leadership in their organizations. It suggests that leadership development may not rest with expensive external programs or even with the best intentions of the human resources department. Rather it may rest with the open-minded recognition that those who appear to rock the boat may turn out to be the most effective of captains.

push against prevailing norms, making a difference in small but steady ways and setting examples from which others can learn. The changes they inspire are so incremental that they barely merit notice—which is exactly why they work so well. Like drops of water, these approaches are innocuous enough in themselves. But over time and in accumulation, they can erode granite.

Consider, for example, how a single individual slowly—but radically—altered the face of his organization. Peter Grant[1] was a black senior executive who held some 18 positions as he moved up the ladder at a large West Coast bank. When he first joined the company as a manager, he was one of only a handful of people of color on the professional staff. Peter had a private, long-term goal: to bring more women and racial minorities into the fold and help them succeed. Throughout his 30-year career running the company's local banks, regional offices, and corporate operations, one of his chief responsibilities was to hire new talent. Each time he had the opportunity, Peter attempted to hire a highly qualified member of a minority. But he did more than that—every time he hired someone, he asked that person to do the same. He explained to the new recruits the importance of hiring women and people of color and why it was their obligation to do likewise.

Whenever minority employees felt frustrated by bias, Peter would act as a supportive mentor. If they threatened to quit, he would talk them out of it. "I know how you feel, but think about the bigger picture here," he'd say. "If you leave, nothing here will change." His example inspired viral behavior in others. Many stayed and hired other minorities; those who didn't carried a commitment to hire minorities into their new companies. By the time Peter retired, more than 3,500 talented minority and female employees had joined the bank.

Peter was the most tempered, yet the most effective, of radicals. For many years, he endured racial slurs and demeaning remarks from colleagues. He waited longer than his peers for promotions; each time he did move up he was told the job was too big for him and he was lucky to have gotten it. "I worked my rear end off to make them comfortable with me," he said, late in his career. "It wasn't *luck*." He was often angry, but lashing out would have been the path of least emotional resistance. So without attacking the system, advancing a bold vision, or wielding great power, Peter chipped away at the organization's demographic base using the full menu of change strategies described below.

Disruptive Self-Expression

At the most tempered end of the change continuum is the kind of self-expression that quietly disrupts others' expectations. Whether waged as a deliberate act of protest or merely as a personal demonstration of one's values, disruptive self-expression in language, dress, office decor, or behavior can slowly change the atmosphere at work. Once people take notice of the expression, they begin to talk about it. Eventually, they may feel brave enough to try the same thing themselves. The more people who talk about the transgressive act or repeat it, the greater the cultural impact.

Consider the case of John Ziwak, a manager in the business development group of a high-growth computer components company. As a hardworking business school graduate who'd landed a plum job, John had every intention of working 80-hour weeks on the fast track to the top. Within a few years, he married a woman who also held a demanding job; soon, he became the father of two. John found his life torn between the competing responsibilities of home and work. To balance the two, John shifted his work hours—coming into the office earlier in the morning so that he could leave by 6 pm. He rarely scheduled late-afternoon meetings and generally refused to take calls at home in the evening between 6:30 and 9. As a result, his family life improved, and he felt much less stress, which in turn improved his performance at work.

At first, John's schedule raised eyebrows; availability was, after all, an unspoken key indicator of commitment to the company. "If John is unwilling to stay past 6," his boss wondered, "is he really committed to his job? Why should I promote him when others are willing and able to work all the time?" But John always met his performance expectations, and his boss didn't want to lose him. Over time, John's colleagues adjusted to his schedule. No one set up conference calls or meetings involving him after 5. One by one, other employees began adopting John's "6 o' clock rule"; calls at home, particularly during dinner hour, took place only when absolutely necessary. Although the 6 o' clock rule was never formalized, it nonetheless became par for the course in John's department. Some of John's colleagues continued to work late, but they all appreciated these changes in work practice and easily accommodated them. Most people in the department felt more, not less, productive during the day as they adapted their work habits to get things done more efficiently—for example, running meetings on schedule and monitoring interruptions in their day. According to John's boss, the employees appreciated the newfound balance in their lives, and productivity in the department did not suffer in the least.

Tempered radicals know that even the smallest forms of disruptive self-expression can be exquisitely powerful. The story of Dr. Frances Conley offers a case in point. By 1987, Dr. Conley had already established herself as a leading researcher and neurosurgeon at Stanford Medical School and the Palo Alto Veteran's Administration hospital. But as one of very few women in the profession, she struggled daily to maintain her feminine identity in a macho profession and her integrity amid gender discrimination. She had to keep her cool when, for example, in the middle of directing a team of residents through complicated brain surgery, a male colleague would stride into the operating room to say, "Move over, honey." "Not only did that undermine my authority and expertise with the team," Dr. Conley recalled later, "but it was unwarranted—and even dangerous. That kind of thing would happen all the time."

Despite the frustration and anger she felt, Dr. Conley at that time had no intention of making a huge issue of her gender. She didn't want the fact that she was a woman to compromise her position, or vice versa. So she expressed herself in all sorts of subtle ways, including in what she wore. Along with her green surgical scrubs, she donned white lace ankle socks—an unequivocal expression of her femininity. In itself, wearing lace ankle socks could hardly be considered a Gandhian act of civil disobedience. The socks merely said, "I can be a neurosurgeon and be feminine." But they spoke loudly enough in the stolid masculinity of the surgical environment, and, along with other small actions on her part, they sparked conversation in the hospital. Nurses and female residents frequently commented on Dr. Conley's style. "She is as demanding as any man and is not afraid to take them on," they would say, in admiration. "But she is also a woman and not ashamed of it."

Ellen Thomas made a comparable statement with her hair. As a young African-American consultant in a technical services business, she navigated constantly between organizational pressures to fit in and her personal desire to challenge norms that made it difficult for her to be herself. So from the beginning of her employment, Ellen expressed herself by wearing her hair in neat cornrow braids.

For Ellen, the way she wore her hair was not just about style; it was a symbol of her racial identity.

Once, before making an important client presentation, a senior colleague advised Ellen to unbraid her hair "to appear more professional." Ellen was miffed, but she didn't respond. Instead, she simply did not comply. Once the presentation was over and the client had been signed, she pulled her colleague aside. "I want you to know why I wear my hair this way," she said calmly. "I'm a black woman, and I happen to like the style. And as you just saw," she smiled, "my hairstyle has nothing to do with my ability to do my job."

Does leaving work at 6 PM or wearing lacy socks or cornrows force immediate change in the culture? Of course not; such acts are too modest. But disruptive self-expression does do two important things. First, it reinforces the tempered radical's sense of the importance of his or her convictions. These acts are self-affirming. Second, it pushes the status quo door slightly ajar by introducing an alternative modus operandi. Whether they are subtle, unspoken, and recognizable by only a few or vocal, visible, and noteworthy to many, such acts, in aggregation, can provoke real reform.

Verbal Jujitsu

Like most martial arts, jujitsu involves taking a force coming at you and redirecting it to change the situation. Employees who practice verbal jujitsu react to undesirable, demeaning statements or actions by turning them into opportunities for change that others will notice.

One form of verbal jujitsu involves calling attention to the opposition's own rhetoric. I recall a story told by a man named Tom Novak, an openly gay executive who worked in the San Francisco offices of a large financial services institution. As Tom and his colleagues began seating themselves around a table for a meeting in a senior executive's large office, the conversation briefly turned to the topic of the upcoming Gay Freedom Day parade and to so-called gay lifestyles in general. Joe, a colleague, said loudly, "I can appreciate

A Spectrum of Tempered Change Strategies

THE TEMPERED RADICAL'S SPECTRUM of strategies is anchored on the left by *disruptive self-expression:* subtle acts of private, individual style. A slightly more public form of expression, *verbal jujitsu,* turns the opposition's negative expression or behavior into opportunities for change. Further along the spectrum, the tempered radical uses *variable-term opportunism* to recognize and act on short- and long-term chances to motivate others. And through *strategic alliance building,* the individual works directly with others to bring about more extensive change. The more conversations an individual's action inspires and the more people it engages, the stronger the impetus toward change becomes.

In reality, people don't apply the strategies in the spectrum sequentially or even necessarily separately. Rather, these tools blur and overlap. Tempered radicals remain flexible in their approach, "heating up" or "cooling off" each as conditions warrant.

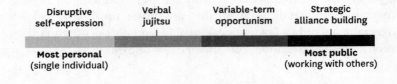

that some people choose a gay lifestyle. I just don't understand why they have to flaunt it in people's faces."

Stung, Tom was tempted to keep his mouth shut and absorb the injury, but that would have left him resentful and angry. He could have openly condemned Joe's bias, but that would have made him look defensive and self-righteous. Instead, he countered Joe with an altered version of Joe's own argument, saying calmly, "I know what you mean, Joe. I'm just wondering about that big picture of your wife on your desk. There's nothing wrong with being straight, but it seems that you are the one announcing your sexuality." Suddenly embarrassed, Joe responded with a simple, "Touché."

Managers can use verbal jujitsu to prevent talented employees, and their valuable contributions, from becoming inadvertently marginalized. That's what happened in the following story. Brad Williams was a sales manager at a high-technology company. During a meeting one day, Brad noticed that Sue, the new marketing director, had tried to interject a few comments, but everything she said was routinely ignored. Brad waited for the right moment to correct the situation. Later on in the meeting, Sue's colleague George raised similar concerns about distributing the new business's products outside the country. The intelligent remark stopped all conversation. During the pause, Brad jumped in: "That's an important idea," he said. "I'm glad George picked up on Sue's concerns. Sue, did George correctly capture what you were thinking?"

With this simple move, Brad accomplished a number of things. First, by indirectly showing how Sue had been silenced and her idea co-opted, he voiced an unspoken fact. Second, by raising Sue's visibility, he changed the power dynamic in the room. Third, his action taught his colleagues a lesson about the way they listened—and didn't. Sue said that after that incident she was no longer passed over in staff meetings.

In practicing verbal jujitsu, both Tom and Brad displayed considerable self-control and emotional intelligence. They listened to and studied the situation at hand, carefully calibrating their responses to disarm without harming. In addition, they identified the underlying issues (sexual bias, the silencing of newcomers) without sounding accusatory and relieved unconscious tensions by voicing them. In so doing, they initiated small but meaningful changes in their colleagues' assumptions and behavior.

Variable-Term Opportunism

Like jazz musicians, who build completely new musical experiences from old standards as they go along, tempered radicals must be creatively open to opportunity. In the short-term, that means being prepared to capitalize on serendipitous circumstances; in the long-term, it often means something more proactive. The first story that follows illustrates the former case; the second is an example of the latter.

Tempered radicals like Chris Morgan know that rich opportunities for reform can often appear suddenly, like a $20 bill found on a sidewalk. An investment manager in the audit department of a New York conglomerate, Chris made a habit of doing whatever he could to reduce waste. To save paper, for example, he would single-space his documents and put them in a smaller font before pressing the "Print" button, and he would use both sides of the paper. One day, Chris noticed that the company cafeteria packaged its sandwiches in Styrofoam boxes that people opened and immediately tossed. He pulled the cafeteria manager aside. "Mary," he said with a big smile, "those turkey-on-focaccia sandwiches look delicious today! I was wondering, though . . . would it be possible to wrap sandwiches only when people asked you to?" By making this very small change, Chris pointed out, the cafeteria would save substantially on packaging costs.

Chris gently rocked the boat by taking the following steps. First, he picked low-hanging fruit, focusing on something that could be done easily and without causing a lot of stir. Next, he attacked the problem not by criticizing Mary's judgment but by enrolling her in his agenda (praising her tempting sandwiches, then making a gentle suggestion). Third, he illuminated the advantages of the proposed change by pointing out the benefits to the cafeteria. And he started a conversation that, through Mary, spread to the rest of the cafeteria staff. Finally, he inspired others to action: Eventually, the cafeteria staff identified and eliminated 12 other wasteful practices.

Add up enough conversations and inspire enough people and, sooner or later, you get real change. A senior executive named Jane Adams offers a case in point. Jane was hired in 1995 to run a 100-person, mostly male software-development division in an extremely fast-growing, pre-IPO technology company. The CEO of the company was an autocrat who expected his employees to emulate his dog-eat-dog management style. Although Jane was new to the job and wanted very much to fit in and succeed, turf wars and command-and-control tactics were anathema to her. Her style was more collaborative; she believed in sharing power. Jane knew that she could not attack the company's culture by arguing with the CEO; rather, she took charge of her own division and ran it her own way. To that end, she took every opportunity to share power with subordinates. She instructed each of her direct reports to delegate responsibility as much as possible. Each time she heard about someone taking initiative in making a decision, she would praise that person openly before his or her manager. She encouraged people to take calculated risks and to challenge her.

When asked to give high-visibility presentations to the company's executive staff, she passed the opportunities to those who had worked directly on the project. At first, senior executives raised their eyebrows, but Jane assured them that the presenter would deliver. Thus, her subordinates gained experience and won credit that, had they worked for someone else, they would likely never have received.

Occasionally, people would tell Jane that they noticed a refreshing contrast between her approach and the company's prevailing one. "Thanks, I'm glad you noticed," she would say with a quiet smile. Within a year, she saw that several of her own direct reports began themselves to lead in a more collaborative manner. Soon, employees from other divisions, hearing that Jane's was one of the best to work for, began requesting transfers. More important, Jane's group became known as one of the best training grounds and Jane as one of the best teachers and mentors of new talent. Nowhere else did people get the experience, responsibility, and confidence that she cultivated in her employees.

For Chris Morgan, opportunity was short-term and serendipitous. For Jane Adams, opportunity was more long-term, something to be mined methodically. In both cases, though, remaining alert to such variable-term opportunities and being ready to capitalize on them were essential.

Strategic Alliance Building

So far, we have seen how tempered radicals, more or less working alone, can effect change. What happens when these individuals work with allies? Clearly, they gain a sense of legitimacy, access to resources and contacts, technical and task assistance, emotional support, and advice. But they gain much more—the power to move issues to the forefront more quickly and directly than they might by working alone.

When one enlists the help of like-minded, similarly tempered coworkers, the strategic alliance gains clout. That's what happened when a group of senior women at a large professional services firm worked with a group of men sympathetic to their cause. The firm's executive management asked the four-woman group to find out why it was so hard for the company to keep female consultants on staff. In the course of their investigation, the women discussed the demanding culture of the firm: a 70-hour work week was the norm, and most consultants spent most of their time on the road, visiting clients. The only people who escaped this demanding schedule were part-time consultants, nearly all of whom happened to be women with families. These part-timers were evaluated according to the same performance criteria—including the expectation of long hours—as full-time workers. Though many of the part-timers were talented contributors, they consistently failed to meet the time criterion and so left the company. To correct the problem, the senior women first gained the ear of several executive men who, they knew, regretted missing time with their own families. The men agreed that this was a problem and that the company could not continue to bleed valuable talent. They signed on to help address the issue and, in a matter of months, the evaluation system was adjusted to make success possible for all workers, regardless of their hours.

Tempered radicals don't allow preconceived notions about "the opposition" to get in their way. Indeed, they understand that those who represent the majority perspective are vitally important to gaining support for their cause. Paul Wielgus quietly started a revolution at his company by effectively persuading the opposition to join him. In 1991, Allied Domecq, the global spirits company whose brands include Courvoisier and Beefeater, hired Paul as a marketing director in its brewing and wholesaling division. Originally founded in 1961 as the result of a merger of three British brewing and pub-owning companies, the company had inherited a bureaucratic culture. Tony

Hales, the CEO, recognized the need for dramatic change inside the organization and appreciated Paul's talent and fresh perspective. He therefore allowed Paul to quit his marketing job, report directly to the CEO, and found a nine-person learning and training department that ran programs to help participants shake off stodgy thinking and boost their creativity. Yet despite the department's blessing from on high and a two-year record of success, some managers thought of it as fluff. In fact, when David, a senior executive from the internal audit department, was asked to review cases of unnecessary expense, he called Paul on the carpet.

Paul's strategy was to treat David not as a threat but as an equal, even a friend. Instead of being defensive during the meeting, Paul used the opportunity to sell his program. He explained that the trainers worked first with individuals to help unearth their personal values, then worked with them in teams to develop new sets of group values that they all believed in. Next, the trainers aligned these personal and departmental values with those of the company as a whole. "You wouldn't believe the changes, David," he said, enthusiastically. "People come out of these workshops feeling so much more excited about their work. They find more meaning and purpose in it, and as a consequence are happier and much more productive. They call in sick less often, they come to work earlier in the morning, and the ideas they produce are much stronger." Once David understood the value of Paul's program, the two began to talk about holding the training program in the internal audit department itself.

Paul's refusal to be frightened by the system, his belief in the importance of his work, his search for creative and collaborative solutions, his lack of defensiveness with an adversary, and his ability to connect with the auditor paved the way for further change at Allied Domecq. Eventually, the working relationship the two men had formed allowed the internal audit department to transform its image as a policing unit into something more positive. The new Audit Services department came to be known as a partner, rather than an enforcer, in the organization as a whole. And as head of the newly renamed department, David became a strong supporter of Paul's work.

Tempered radicals understand that people who represent the majority perspective can be important allies in more subtle ways as well. In navigating the course between their desire to undo the status quo and the organizational requirements to uphold it, tempered radicals benefit from the advice of insiders who know just how hard to push. When a feminist who wants to change the way her company treats women befriends a conservative Republican man, she knows he can warn her of political minefields. When a Latino manager wants his company to put a Spanish-language version of a manual up on the company's intranet, he knows that the white, monolingual executive who runs operations may turn out to be an excellent advocate.

Of course, tempered radicals know that not everyone is an ally, but they also know it's pointless to see those who represent the status quo as enemies. The senior women found fault with an inequitable evaluation system, not with their male colleagues. Paul won David's help by giving him the benefit of the doubt from the very beginning of their relationship. Indeed, tempered radicals constantly consider all possible courses of action: "Under what conditions, for what issues, and in what circumstances does it make sense to join forces with others?"; "How can I best use this alliance to support my efforts?"

Clearly, there is no one right way to effect change. What works for one individual under one set of circumstances may not work for others under different conditions. The examples above illustrate how tempered radicals use a spectrum of quiet approaches to change their organizations. Some actions are small, private, and muted; some are larger and more public. Their influence spreads as they recruit others and spawn conversations. Top managers can learn a lot from these people about the mechanics of evolutionary change.

Tempered radicals bear no banners; they sound no trumpets. Their ends are sweeping, but their means are mundane. They are firm in their commitments, yet flexible in the ways they fulfill them. Their actions may be small but can spread like a virus. They yearn for rapid change but trust in patience. They often work individually yet pull people together. Instead of stridently pressing their agendas, they start conversations. Rather than battling powerful foes, they seek powerful friends. And in the face of setbacks, they keep going. To do all this, tempered radicals understand revolutionary change for what it is—a phenomenon that can occur suddenly but more often than not requires time, commitment, and the patience to endure.

Originally published in October 2001. Reprint 7923

Notes

1. With the exception of those in the VA hospital and Allied Domecq cases, all the names used through this article are fictitious.

Tipping Point Leadership

by W. Chan Kim and Renée Mauborgne

IN FEBRUARY 1994, William Bratton was appointed police commissioner of New York City. The odds were against him. The New York Police Department, with a $2 billion budget and a workforce of 35,000 police officers, was notoriously difficult to manage. Turf wars over jurisdiction and funding were rife. Officers were underpaid relative to their counterparts in neighboring communities, and promotion seemed to bear little relationship to performance. Crime had gotten so far out of control that the press referred to the Big Apple as the Rotten Apple. Indeed, many social scientists had concluded, after three decades of increases, that New York City crime was impervious to police intervention. The best the police could do was react to crimes once they were committed.

Yet in less than two years, and without an increase in his budget, Bill Bratton turned New York into the safest large city in the nation. Between 1994 and 1996, felony crime fell 39%; murders, 50%; and theft, 35%. Gallup polls reported that public confidence in the NYPD jumped from 37% to 73%, even as internal surveys showed job satisfaction in the police department reaching an all-time high. Not surprisingly, Bratton's popularity soared, and in 1996, he was featured on the cover of *Time*. Perhaps most impressive, the changes have outlasted their instigator, implying a fundamental shift in the department's organizational culture and strategy. Crime rates have continued to fall: Statistics released in December 2002 revealed that New York's overall crime rate is the lowest among the 25 largest cities in the United States.

The NYPD turnaround would be impressive enough for any police chief. For Bratton, though, it is only the latest of no fewer than five successful turnarounds in a 20-year career in policing. In the hope that Bratton can repeat his New York and Boston successes, Los Angeles has recruited him to take on the challenge of turning around the LAPD. (For a summary of his achievements, see the table "Bratton in action.")

So what makes Bill Bratton tick? As management researchers, we have long been fascinated by what triggers high performance or suddenly brings an ailing organization back to life. In an effort to find the common elements underlying such leaps in performance, we have built a database of more than 125 business and nonbusiness organizations. Bratton first caught our attention in the early 1990s, when we heard about his turnaround of the New York Transit Police. Bratton was special for us because in all of his turnarounds, he succeeded in record time despite facing all four of the hurdles that managers consistently claim block high performance: an organization wedded to the status quo, limited resources, a demotivated staff, and opposition from powerful vested interests. If Bratton could succeed against these odds, other leaders, we reasoned, could learn a lot from him.

Over the years, through our professional and personal networks and the rich public information available on the police sector, we have systematically compared the strategic, managerial, and performance records of Bratton's turnarounds. We have followed up by interviewing the key players, including Bratton himself, as well as many other people who for professional—or sometimes personal—reasons tracked the events.

Our research led us to conclude that all of Bratton's turnarounds are textbook examples of what we call tipping point leadership. The theory of tipping points, which has its roots in epidemiology, is well known; it hinges on the insight that in any organization, once the beliefs and energies of a critical mass of people are engaged, conversion to a new idea will spread like an epidemic, bringing about

Idea in Brief

How can you overcome the hurdles facing any organization struggling to change: addiction to the status quo, limited resources, demotivated employees, and opposition from powerful vested interests?

Take lessons from police chief Bill Bratton, who's pulled the trick off five times. Most dramatically, he transformed the U.S.'s most dangerous city—New York—into its safest. Bratton used **tipping point leadership** to make unarguable calls for change, concentrate resources on what really mattered, mobilize key players' commitment, and silence naysayers.

Not every executive has Bratton's personality, but most have his potential—if they follow his success formula.

fundamental change very quickly. The theory suggests that such a movement can be unleashed only by agents who make unforgettable and unarguable calls for change, who concentrate their resources on what really matters, who mobilize the commitment of the organization's key players, and who succeed in silencing the most vocal naysayers. Bratton did all of these things in all of his turnarounds.

Most managers only dream of pulling off the kind of performance leaps Bratton delivered. Even Jack Welch needed some ten years and tens of millions of dollars of restructuring and training to turn GE into the powerhouse it is today. Few CEOs have the time and money that Welch had, and most—even those attempting relatively mild change—are soon daunted by the scale of the hurdles they face. Yet we have found that the dream can indeed become a reality. For what makes Bratton's turnarounds especially exciting to us is that his approach to overcoming the hurdles standing in the way of high performance has been remarkably consistent. His successes, therefore, are not just a matter of personality but also of method, which suggests that they can be replicated. Tipping point leadership is learnable.

In the following pages, we'll lay out the approach that has enabled Bratton to overcome the forces of inertia and reach the tipping point. We'll show first how Bratton overcame the cognitive hurdles that block companies from recognizing the need for radical

Idea in Practice

Four Steps to the Tipping Point

1. Break through the cognitive hurdle.

To make a compelling case for change, don't just point at the numbers and demand better ones. Your abstract message won't stick. Instead, make key managers *experience* your organization's problems.

> *Example:* New Yorkers once viewed subways as the most dangerous places in their city. But the New York Transit Police's senior staff pooh-poohed public fears—because none had ever ridden subways. To shatter their complacency, Bratton required all NYTP officers—himself included—to commute by subway. Seeing the jammed turnstiles, youth gangs, and derelicts, they grasped the need for change—and embraced responsibility for it.

2. Sidestep the resource hurdle.

Rather than trimming your ambitions (dooming your company to mediocrity) or fighting for more resources (draining attention from the underlying problems), concentrate *current* resources on areas *most* needing change.

> *Example:* Since the majority of subway crimes occurred at only a few stations, Bratton focused manpower there—instead of putting a cop on every subway line, entrance, and exit.

3. Jump the motivational hurdle.

To turn a mere strategy into a movement, people must recognize what needs to be done and yearn to do it themselves. But don't try reforming your whole organization; that's cumbersome and expensive. Instead, motivate *key influencers*—persuasive

change. Then we'll describe how he successfully managed around the public sector's endemic constraints on resources, which he even turned to his advantage. In the third section, we'll explain how Bratton overcame the motivational hurdles that had discouraged and demoralized even the most eager police officers. Finally, we'll describe how Bratton neatly closed off potentially fatal resistance from vocal and powerful opponents. (For a graphic summary of the ideas expressed in this article, see the figure "Tipping point leadership at a glance.")

people with multiple connections. Like bowling kingpins hit straight on, they topple all the other pins. Most organizations have several key influencers who share common problems and concerns—making it easy to identify and motivate them.

Example: Bratton put the NYPD's key influencers—precinct commanders—under a spotlight during semiweekly crime strategy review meetings, where peers and superiors grilled commanders about precinct performance. Results? A culture of performance, accountability, and learning that commanders replicated down the ranks.

Also make challenges attainable. Bratton exhorted staff to make NYC's streets safe "block by block, precinct by precinct, and borough by borough."

4. Knock over the political hurdle.

Even when organizations reach their tipping points, powerful vested interests resist change. Identify and silence key naysayers early by putting a respected senior insider on your top team.

Example: At the NYPD, Bratton appointed 20-year veteran cop John Timoney as his number two. Timoney knew the key players and how they played the political game. Early on, he identified likely saboteurs and resisters among top staff—prompting a changing of the guard.

Also, silence opposition with indisputable facts. When Bratton proved his proposed crime-reporting system required less than 18 minutes a day, time-crunched precinct commanders adopted it.

Break Through the Cognitive Hurdle

In many turnarounds, the hardest battle is simply getting people to agree on the causes of current problems and the need for change. Most CEOs try to make the case for change simply by pointing to the numbers and insisting that the company achieve better ones. But messages communicated through numbers seldom stick. To the line managers—the very people the CEO needs to win over—the case for change seems abstract and remote. Those whose units are doing well feel that the criticism is not directed at them, that the problem

Bratton in action

The New York Police Department was not Bill Bratton's first turnaround. The table describes his biggest challenges and achievements during his 20 years as a policy reformer.

Domain	Boston Police District 4	Massachusetts Bay Transit Authority (MBTA)	Boston Metropolitan Police ("The Mets")	New York Transit Police (NYTP)	New York Police Department (NYPD)
Years	1977–1982	1983–1986	1986–1990	1990–1992	1994–1996
Position	Sergeant, lieutenant	Superintendent	Superintendent	Chief of police	Commissioner
Setting	Assaults, drug dealing, prostitution, public drinking, and graffiti were endemic to the area. The Boston public shied away from attending baseball games and other events and from shopping in the Fenway neighborhood for fear of being robbed or attacked or having their cars stolen.	Subway crime had been on the rise for the past five years. The media dubbed the Boston subway the Terror Train. The *Boston Globe* published a series on police incompetence in the MBTA.	The Mets lacked modern equipment, procedures, and discipline. Physical facilities were crumbling. Accountability, discipline, and morale were low in the 600-person Mets workforce.	Crime had risen 25% per year in the past three years—twice the overall rate for the city. Subway use by the public had declined sharply; polls indicated that New Yorkers considered the subway the most dangerous place in the city. There were 170,000 fare evaders per day, costing the city $80 million annually. Aggressive panhandling and vandalism were endemic. More than 5,000 people were living in the subway system.	The middle class was fleeing to the suburbs in search of a better quality of life. There was public despair in the face of the high crime rate. Crime was seen as part of a breakdown of social norms. The budget for policing was shrinking. The NYPD budget (aside from personnel) was being cut by 35%. The staff was demoralized and relatively underpaid.

Domain	Boston Police District 4	Massachu-setts Bay Transit Authority (MBTA)	Boston Metropolitan Police ("The Mets")	New York Transit Police (NYTP)	New York Police Depart-ment (NYPD)
Results	Crime throughout the Fenway area was dramatically reduced. Tourists, residents, and investment returned as an entire area of the city rebounded.	Crime on the MBTA decreased by 27%; arrests rose to 1,600 per year from 600. The MBTA police met more than 800 standards of excellence to be accredited by the National Commission on Accreditation for Police Agencies. It was only the 13th police department in the country to meet this standard. Equipment acquired during his tenure: 55 new mid-size cars, new uniforms, and new logos. Ridership began to grow.	Employee morale rose as Bratton instilled accountability, protocol, and pride. In three years, the Metropolitan Police changed from a dispirited, do-nothing, reactive organization with a poor self-image and an even worse public image to a very proud, proactive department. Equipment acquired during his tenure: 100 new vehicles, a helicopter, and a state-of-the-art radio system.	In two years, Bratton reduced felony crime by 22%, with robberies down by 40%. Increased confidence in the subway led to increased ridership. Fare evasion was cut in half. Equipment acquired during his tenure: a state-of-the-art communication system, advanced handguns for officers, and new patrol cars (the number of cars doubled).	Overall crime fell by 17%. Felony crime fell by 39%. Murders fell by 50%. Theft fell by 35% (robberies were down by one-third, burglaries by one-quarter). There were 200,000 fewer victims a year than in 1990. By the end of Bratton's tenure, the NYPD had a 73% positive rating, up from 37% four years earlier.

is top management's. Managers of poorly performing units feel that they have been put on notice—and people worried about job security are more likely to be scanning the job market than trying to solve the company's problems.

For all these reasons, tipping point leaders like Bratton do not rely on numbers to break through the organization's cognitive hurdles.

Instead, they put their key managers face-to-face with the operational problems so that the managers cannot evade reality. Poor performance becomes something they witness rather than hear about. Communicating in this way means that the message—performance is poor and needs to be fixed—sticks with people, which is essential if they are to be convinced not only that a turnaround is necessary but that it is something they can achieve.

When Bratton first went to New York to head the transit police in April 1990, he discovered that none of the senior staff officers rode the subway. They commuted to work and traveled around in cars provided by the city. Comfortably removed from the facts of underground life—and reassured by statistics showing that only 3% of the city's major crimes were committed in the subway—the senior managers had little sensitivity to riders' widespread concern about safety. In order to shatter the staff's complacency, Bratton began requiring that all transit police officials—beginning with himself—ride the subway to work, to meetings, and at night. It was many staff officers' first occasion in years to share the ordinary citizen's subway experience and see the situation their subordinates were up against: jammed turnstiles, aggressive beggars, gangs of youths jumping turnstiles and jostling people on the platforms, winos and homeless people sprawled on benches. It was clear that even if few major crimes took place in the subway, the whole place reeked of fear and disorder. With that ugly reality staring them in the face, the transit force's senior managers could no longer deny the need for a change in their policing methods.

Bratton uses a similar approach to help sensitize his superiors to his problems. For instance, when he was running the police division of the Massachusetts Bay Transit Authority (MBTA), which runs the Boston-area subway and buses, the transit authority's board decided to purchase small squad cars that would be cheaper to buy and run. Instead of fighting the decision, Bratton invited the MBTA's general manager for a tour of the district. He picked him up in a small car just like the ones that were to be ordered. He jammed the seats forward to let the general manager feel how little legroom a six-foot cop would have, then drove him over every pothole he could find. Brat-

Tipping point leadership at a glance

Leaders like Bill Bratton use a four-step process to bring about rapid, dramatic, and lasting change with limited resources. The cognitive and resource hurdles shown here represent the obstacles that organizations face in reorienting and formulating strategy. The motivational and political hurdles prevent a strategy's rapid execution. Tipping all four hurdles leads to rapid strategy reorientation and execution. Overcoming these hurdles is, of course, a continuous process because the innovation of today soon becomes the conventional norm of tomorrow.

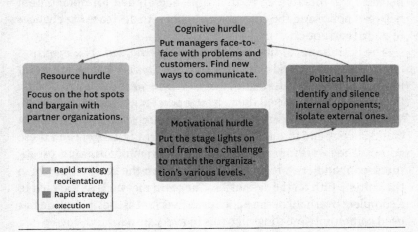

ton also put on his belt, cuffs, and gun for the trip so the general manager could see how little space there was for the tools of the officer's trade. After just two hours, the general manager wanted out. He said he didn't know how Bratton could stand being in such a cramped car for so long on his own—let alone if there were a criminal in the backseat. Bratton got the larger cars he wanted.

Bratton reinforces direct experiences by insisting that his officers meet the communities they are protecting. The feedback is often revealing. In the late 1970s, Boston's Police District 4, which included Symphony Hall, the Christian Science Mother Church, and other cultural institutions, was experiencing a surge in crime. The public was increasingly intimidated; residents were selling and leaving, pushing the community into a downward spiral. The Boston police performance statistics, however, did not reflect this reality. District 4 police, it seemed, were doing a splendid job of rapidly clearing 911 calls and tracking down perpetrators of serious crimes. To solve this paradox, Bratton had the unit organize community meetings in schoolrooms and civic centers so that citizens could voice their concerns to district sergeants and detectives. Obvious as the logic of this practice sounds, it was the first time in Boston's police history that anyone had attempted such an initiative—mainly because the practice up to that time had argued for detachment between police and the community in order to decrease the chances of police corruption.

The limitations of that practice quickly emerged. The meetings began with a show-and-tell by the officers: This is what we are work- ing on and why. But afterward, when citizens were invited to discuss the issues that concerned them, a huge perception gap came to light. While the police officers took pride in solving serious offenses like grand larceny and murder, few citizens felt in any danger from these crimes. They were more troubled by constant minor irritants: prosti- tutes, panhandlers, broken-down cars left on the streets, drunks in the gutters, filth on the sidewalks. The town meetings quickly led to a complete overhaul of the police priorities for District 4. Bratton has used community meetings like this in every turnaround since.

Bratton's internal communications strategy also plays an impor- tant role in breaking through the cognitive hurdles. Traditionally, internal police communication is largely based on memos, staff bul- letins, and other documents. Bratton knows that few police officers have the time or inclination to do more than throw these documents into the wastebasket. Officers rely instead on rumor and media sto- ries for insights into what headquarters is up to. So Bratton typically calls on the help of expert communication outsiders. In New York, for instance, he recruited John Miller, an investigative television reporter known for his gutsy and innovative style, as his communi- cation czar. Miller arranged for Bratton to communicate through video messages that were played at roll calls, which had the effect of bringing Bratton—and his opinions—closer to the people he had to win over. At the same time, Miller's journalistic savvy made it easier for the NYPD to ensure that press interviews and stories echoed the strong internal messages Bratton was sending.

Sidestep the Resource Hurdle

Once people in an organization accept the need for change and more or less agree on what needs to be done, leaders are often faced with the stark reality of limited resources. Do they have the money for the necessary changes? Most reformist CEOs do one of two things at this point. They trim their ambitions, dooming the company to mediocrity at best and demoralizing the workforce all over again, or they fight for more resources from their bankers and shareholders, a process that can take time and divert attention from the underlying problems.

That trap is completely avoidable. Leaders like Bratton know how to reach the organization's tipping point without extra resources. They can achieve a great deal with the resources they have. What they do is concentrate their resources on the places that are most in need of change and that have the biggest possible payoffs. This idea, in fact, is at the heart of Bratton's famous (and once hotly debated) philosophy of zero-tolerance policing.

Having won people over to the idea of change, Bratton must persuade them to take a cold look at what precisely is wrong with their operating practices. It is at this point that he turns to the numbers, which he is adept at using to force through major changes. Take the case of the New York narcotics unit. Bratton's predecessors had treated it as secondary in importance, partly because they assumed that responding to 911 calls was the top priority. As a result, less than 5% of the NYPD's manpower was dedicated to fighting narcotics crimes.

At an initial meeting with the NYPD's chiefs, Bratton's deputy commissioner of crime strategy, Jack Maple, asked people around the table for their estimates of the percentage of crimes attributable to narcotics use. Most said 50%; others, 70%; the lowest estimate was 30%. On that basis, a narcotics unit consisting of less than 5% of the police force was grossly understaffed, Maple pointed out. What's

The strategy canvas of transit:

How Bratton refocused resources

In comparing strategies across companies, we like to use a tool we call the strategy canvas, which highlights differences in strategies and resource allocation. The strategy canvas shown here compares the strategy and allocation of resources of the New York Transit Police before and after Bill Bratton's appointment as chief. The vertical axis shows the relative level of resource allocation. The horizontal axis shows the various elements of strategy in which the investments were made. Although a dramatic shift in resource allocation occurred and performance rose dramatically, overall investment of resources remained more or less constant. Bratton did this by de-emphasizing or virtually eliminating some traditional features of transit police work while increasing emphasis on others or creating new ones. For example, he was able to reduce the time police officers spent processing suspects by introducing mobile processing centers known as "bust buses."

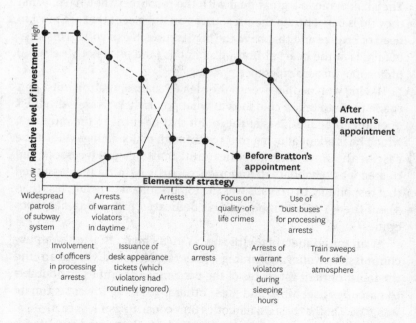

more, it turned out that the narcotics squad largely worked Monday through Friday, even though drugs were sold in large quantities— and drug-related crimes persistently occurred—on the weekends. Why the weekday schedule? Because it had always been done that way; it was an unquestioned modus operandi. Once these facts were presented, Bratton's call for a major reallocation of staff and resources within the NYPD was quickly accepted.

A careful examination of the facts can also reveal where changes in key policies can reduce the need for resources, as Bratton demonstrated during his tenure as chief of New York's transit police. His predecessors had lobbied hard for the money to increase the number of subway cops, arguing that the only way to stop muggers was to have officers ride every subway line and patrol each of the system's 700 exits and entrances. Bratton, by contrast, believed that subway crime could be resolved not by throwing more resources at the problem but by better targeting those resources. To prove the point, he had members of his staff analyze where subway crimes were being committed. They found that the vast majority occurred at only a few stations and on a couple of lines, which suggested that a targeted strategy would work well. At the same time, he shifted more of the force out of uniform and into plain clothes at the hot spots. Criminals soon realized that an absence of uniforms did not necessarily mean an absence of cops.

Distribution of officers was not the only problem. Bratton's analysis revealed that an inordinate amount of police time was wasted in processing arrests. It took an officer up to 16 hours per arrest to book the suspect and file papers on the incident. What's more, the officers so hated the bureaucratic process that they avoided making arrests in minor cases. Bratton realized that he could dramatically increase his available policing resources—not to mention the officers' motivation—if he could somehow improvise around this problem. His solution was to park "bust buses"—old buses converted into arrest-processing centers—around the corner from targeted subway stations. Processing time was cut from 16 hours to just one. Innovations like that enabled Bratton to dramatically reduce subway crime—even without an increase in the number of officers on duty at any given time. (The figure "The strategy canvas of transit: How Bratton refocused resources" illustrates how radically Bratton refocused the transit police's resources.)

Bratton's drive for data-driven policing solutions led to the creation of the famous Compstat crime database. The database, used to identify hot spots for intense police intervention, captures weekly crime and arrest activity—including times, locations, and associated enforcement activities—at the precinct, borough, and city levels. The Compstat reports allowed Bratton and the entire police department to easily discern established and emerging hot spots for efficient resource targeting and retargeting.

In addition to refocusing the resources he already controls, Bratton has proved adept at trading resources he doesn't need for those he does. The chiefs of public-sector organizations are reluctant to advertise excess resources, let alone lend them to other agencies, because acknowledged excess resources tend to get reallocated. So over time, some organizations end up well endowed with resources they don't need—even if they are short of others. When Bratton took over as chief of the transit police, for example, his general counsel and policy adviser, Dean Esserman, now police chief of Providence, Rhode Island, discovered that the transit unit had more unmarked cars than it needed but was starved of office space. The New York Division of Parole, on the other hand, was short of cars but had excess office space. Esserman and Bratton offered the obvious trade. It was gratefully accepted by the parole division, and transit officials were delighted to get the first floor of a prime downtown building. The deal stoked Bratton's credibility within the organization, which would make it easier for him to introduce more fundamental changes later, and it marked him, to his political bosses, as a man who could solve problems.

Jump the Motivational Hurdle

Alerting employees to the need for change and identifying how it can be achieved with limited resources are necessary for reaching an organization's tipping point. But if a new strategy is to become a movement, employees must not only recognize what needs to be done, they must also want to do it. Many CEOs recognize the importance of getting people motivated to make changes, but they make the mistake of trying to reform incentives throughout the whole organization. That process takes a long time to implement and can prove very expensive, given the wide variety of motivational needs in any large company.

One way Bratton solves the motivation problem is by singling out the key influencers—people inside or outside the organization with disproportionate power due to their connections with the organization, their ability to persuade, or their ability to block access to resources. Bratton recognizes that these influencers act like kingpins in bowling: When you hit them just right, all the pins topple over. Getting the key influencers motivated frees an organization from having to motivate everyone, yet everyone in the end is touched and changed. And because most organizations have relatively small numbers of key influencers, and those people tend to share common problems and concerns, it is relatively easy for CEOs to identify and motivate them.

Bratton's approach to motivating his key influencers is to put them under a spotlight. Perhaps his most significant reform of the NYPD's operating practices was instituting a semiweekly strategy review meeting that brought the top brass together with the city's 76 precinct commanders. Bratton had identified the commanders as key influential people in the NYPD, because each one directly managed 200 to 400 officers. Attendance was mandatory for all senior staff, including three-star chiefs, deputy commissioners, and borough chiefs. Bratton was there as often as possible.

At the meetings, which took place in an auditorium at the police command center, a selected precinct commander was called before a panel of the senior staff (the selected officer was given only two days' notice, in order to keep all the commanders on their toes). The commander in the spotlight was questioned by both the panel and other commanders about the precinct's performance. He or she was responsible for explaining projected maps and charts that showed, based on the Compstat data, the precinct's patterns of crimes and when and where the police responded. The commander would be required to provide a detailed explanation if police activity did not mirror crime spikes and would also be asked how officers were addressing the precinct's issues and why performance was improving or deteriorating. The meetings allowed Bratton and his senior staff to carefully monitor and assess how well commanders were motivating and managing their people and how well they were focusing on strategic hot spots.

The meetings changed the NYPD's culture in several ways. By making results and responsibilities clear to everyone, the meetings helped to introduce a culture of performance. Indeed, a photo of the commander who was about to be grilled appeared on the front page of the handout that each meeting participant received, emphasizing that the commander was accountable for the precinct's results. An incompetent commander could no longer cover up his failings by blaming his precinct's results on the shortcomings of neighboring precincts, because his neighbors were in the room and could respond. By the same token, the meetings gave high achievers a chance to be recognized both for making improvements in their own precincts and for helping other commanders. The meetings also allowed police leaders to compare notes on their experiences; before Bratton's arrival, precinct commanders hardly ever got together as a group. Over time, this management style filtered down through the ranks, as the precinct commanders tried out their own versions of Bratton's meetings. With the spotlight shining brightly on their performance, the commanders were highly motivated to get all the officers under their control marching to the new strategy.

The great challenges in applying this kind of motivational device, of course, are ensuring that people feel it is based on fair processes and seeing to it that they can draw lessons from both good and bad results. Doing so increases the organization's collective strength and everyone's chance of winning. Bratton addresses the issue of fair process by engaging all key influencers in the procedures, setting clear performance expectations, and explaining why these strategy meetings, for example, are essential for fast execution of policy.

He addresses the issue of learning by insisting that the team of top brass play an active role in meetings and by being an active moderator himself. Precinct commanders can talk about their achievements or failures without feeling that they are showing off or being shown up. Successful commanders aren't seen as bragging, because it's clear to everyone that they were asked by Bratton's top team to show, in detail, how they achieved their successes. And for commanders on the receiving end, the sting of having to be taught a lesson by a colleague is mitigated, at least, by their not having to suffer the indignity of asking for it. Bratton's popularity soared when he created a humorous video satirizing the grilling that precinct commanders were given; it showed the cops that he understood just how much he was asking of them.

Bratton also uses another motivational lever: framing the reform challenge itself. Framing the challenge is one of the most subtle and sensitive tasks of the tipping point leader; unless people believe that results are attainable, a turnaround is unlikely to succeed. On the face of it, Bratton's goal in New York was so ambitious as to be scarcely believable. Who would believe that the city could be made one of the safest in the country? And who would want to invest time and energy in chasing such an impossible dream?

To make the challenge seem manageable, Bratton framed it as a series of specific goals that officers at different levels could relate to. As he put it, the challenge the NYPD faced was to make the streets of New York safe "block by block, precinct by precinct, and borough by borough." Thus framed, the task was both all encompassing and doable. For the cops on the street, the challenge was making their beats or blocks safe—no more. For the commanders, the challenge was making their precincts safe—no more. Borough heads also had a concrete goal within their capabilities: making their boroughs safe—no more. No matter what their positions, officers couldn't say that what was being asked of them was too tough. Nor could they claim that achieving it was out of their hands. In this way, responsibility for the turnaround shifted from Bratton to each of the thousands of police officers on the force.

Knock Over the Political Hurdle

Organizational politics is an inescapable reality in public and corporate life, a lesson Bratton learned the hard way. In 1980, at age 34 one of the youngest lieutenants in Boston's police department, he had proudly put up a plaque in his office that said: "Youth and skill will win out every time over age and treachery." Within just a few months, having been shunted into a dead-end position due to a mixture of office politics and his own brashness, Bratton took the sign down. He never again forgot the importance of understanding the plotting, intrigue, and politics involved in pushing through change. Even if an organization has reached the tipping point, powerful vested interests will resist the impending reforms. The more likely change becomes, the more fiercely and vocally these negative influencers—both internal and external—will fight to protect their positions, and their resistance can seriously damage, even derail, the reform process.

Bratton anticipates these dangers by identifying and silencing powerful naysayers early on. To that end, he always ensures that he has a respected senior insider on the top team. At the NYPD, for instance, Bratton appointed John Timoney, now Miami's police commissioner, as his number two. Timoney was a cop's cop, respected and feared for his dedication to the NYPD and for the more than 60 decorations he had received. Twenty years in the ranks had taught him who all the key players were and how they played the political game. One of the first tasks Timoney carried out was to report to Bratton on the likely attitudes of the top staff toward Bratton's concept of zero-tolerance policing, identifying those who would fight or silently sabotage the new initiatives. This led to a dramatic changing of the guard.

Of course, not all naysayers should face the ultimate sanction— there might not be enough people left to man the barricades. In many cases, therefore, Bratton silences opposition by example and indisputable fact. For instance, when first asked to compile detailed crime maps and information packages for the strategy review meetings, most precinct commanders complained that the task would take too long and waste valuable police time that could be better spent fighting crime. Anticipating this argument, deputy commissioner Jack Maple set up a reporting system that covered the city's most crime-ridden areas. Operating the system required no more than 18 minutes a day, which worked out, as he told the precinct commanders, to less than 1% of the average precinct's workload. Try to argue with that.

Often the most serious opposition to reform comes from outside. In the public sector, as in business, an organization's change of strategy has an impact on other organizations—partners and competitors alike. The change is likely to be resisted by those players if they are happy with the status quo and powerful enough to protest the changes. Bratton's strategy for dealing with such opponents is to isolate them by building a broad coalition with the other independent powers in his realm. In New York, for example, one of the most serious threats to his reforms came from the city's courts, which were concerned that zero-tolerance policing would result in an enormous number of small-crimes cases clogging the court schedule.

To get past the opposition of the courts, Bratton solicited the support of no less a personage than the mayor, Rudolph Giuliani, who had considerable influence over the district attorneys, the courts, and the city jail on Rikers Island. Bratton's team demonstrated to the mayor that the court system had the capacity to handle minor "quality of life" crimes, even though doing so would presumably not be palatable for them.

The mayor decided to intervene. While conceding to the courts that a crackdown campaign would cause a short-term spike in court work, he also made clear that he and the NYPD believed it would eventually lead to a workload reduction for the courts. Working together in this way, Bratton and the mayor were able to maneuver the courts into processing quality-of-life crimes. Seeing that the mayor was aligned with Bratton, the courts appealed to the city's legislators, advocating legislation to exempt them from handling minor-crime cases on the grounds that such cases would clog the system and entail significant costs to the city. Bratton and the mayor, who were holding weekly strategy meetings, added another ally to their coalition by placing their case before the press, in particular the *New York Times*. Through a series of press conferences and articles and at every interview opportunity, the issue of zero tolerance was put at the front and center of public debate with a clear, simple message: If the courts did not help crack down on quality-of-life crimes, the city's crime rates would not improve. It was a matter not of saving dollars but of saving the city.

Bratton's alliance with the mayor's office and the city's leading media institution successfully isolated the courts. The courts could hardly be seen as publicly opposing an initiative that would not only make New York a more attractive place to live but would ultimately reduce the number of cases brought before them. With the mayor speaking aggressively in the press about the need to pursue quality-of-life crimes and the city's most respected—and liberal—newspaper giving credence to the policy, the costs of fighting Bratton's strategy were daunting. Thanks to this savvy politicking, one of Bratton's biggest battles was won, and the legislation was not enacted. The courts would handle quality-of-life crimes. In due course, the crime rates did indeed come tumbling down.

Of course, Bill Bratton, like any leader, must share the credit for his successes. Turning around an organization as large and as wedded to the status quo as the NYPD requires a collective effort. But the tipping point would not have been reached without him—or another leader like him. And while we recognize that not every executive has the personality to be a Bill Bratton, there are many who have that potential once they know the formula for success. It is that formula that we have tried to present, and we urge managers who wish to turn their companies around, but have limited time and resources, to take note. By addressing the hurdles to tipping point change described in these pages, they will stand a chance of achieving the same kind of results for their shareholders as Bratton has delivered to the citizens of New York.

Originally published in April 2003. Reprint R0304D

A Survival Guide for Leaders

by Ronald A. Heifetz and Marty Linsky

THINK OF THE MANY top executives in recent years who, sometimes after long periods of considerable success, have crashed and burned. Or think of individuals you have known in less prominent positions, perhaps people spearheading significant change initiatives in their organizations, who have suddenly found themselves out of a job. Think about yourself: In exercising leadership, have *you* ever been removed or pushed aside?

Let's face it, to lead is to live dangerously. While leadership is often depicted as an exciting and glamorous endeavor, one in which you inspire others to follow you through good times and bad, such a portrayal ignores leadership's dark side: the inevitable attempts to take you out of the game.

Those attempts are sometimes justified. People in top positions must often pay the price for a flawed strategy or a series of bad decisions. But frequently, something more is at work. We're not talking here about conventional office politics; we're talking about the high-stake risks you face whenever you try to lead an organization through difficult but necessary change. The risks during such times are especially high because change that truly transforms an organization, be it a multibillion-dollar company or a ten-person sales team, demands that people give up things they hold dear: daily habits, loyalties, ways of thinking. In return for these sacrifices, they may be offered nothing more than the possibility of a better future.

We refer to this kind of wrenching organizational transformation as "adaptive change," something very different from the "technical change" that occupies people in positions of authority on a regular basis. Technical problems, while often challenging, can be solved applying existing know-how and the organization's current problem-solving processes. Adaptive problems resist these kinds of solutions because they require individuals throughout the organization to alter their ways; as the people themselves are the problem, the solution lies with them. (See the sidebar "Adaptive Versus Technical Change: Whose Problem Is It?") Responding to an adaptive challenge with a technical fix may have some short-term appeal. But to make real progress, sooner or later those who lead must ask themselves and the people in the organization to face a set of deeper issues—and to accept a solution that may require turning part or all of the organization upside down.

It is at this point that danger lurks. And most people who lead in such a situation—swept up in the action, championing a cause they believe in—are caught unawares. Over and over again, we have seen courageous souls blissfully ignorant of an approaching threat until it was too late to respond.

The hazard can take numerous forms. You may be attacked directly in an attempt to shift the debate to your character and style and avoid discussion of your initiative. You may be marginalized, forced into the position of becoming so identified with one issue that your broad authority is undermined. You may be seduced by your supporters and, fearful of losing their approval and affection, fail to demand they make the sacrifices needed for the initiative to succeed. You may be diverted from your goal by people overwhelming you with the day-to-day details of carrying it out, keeping you busy and preoccupied.

Each one of these thwarting tactics—whether done consciously or not—grows out of people's aversion to the organizational disequilibrium created by your initiative. By attempting to undercut you, people strive to restore order, maintain what is familiar to them, and protect themselves from the pains of adaptive change. They want to be comfortable again, and you're in the way.

Idea in Brief

It's exciting—even glamorous—to lead others through good times and bad. But leadership also has its dark side: the inevitable attempts to take you out of the game when you're steering your organization through difficult change.

Leading change requires asking people to confront painful issues and give up habits and beliefs they hold dear. Result? Some people try to eliminate change's visible agent—you. Whether they attack you personally, undermine your authority, or seduce you into seeing things their way, their goal is the same: to derail you, easing *their* pain and restoring familiar order.

How to resist attempts to remove you—and continue to propel change forward? Manage your hostile *environment*—your organization and its people—and your own *vulnerabilities*.

So how do you protect yourself? Over a combined 50 years of teaching and consulting, we have asked ourselves that question time and again—usually while watching top-notch and well-intentioned folks get taken out of the game. On occasion, the question has become painfully personal; we as individuals have been knocked off course or out of the action more than once in our own leadership efforts. So we are offering what we hope are some pragmatic answers that grow out of these observations and experiences. We should note that while our advice clearly applies to senior executives, it also applies to people trying to lead change initiatives from positions of little or no formal organizational authority.

This "survival guide" has two main parts. The first looks outward, offering tactical advice about relating to your organization and the people in it. It is designed to protect you from those trying to push you aside before you complete your initiative. The second looks inward, focusing on your own human needs and vulnerabilities. It is designed to keep you from bringing yourself down.

A Hostile Environment

Leading major organizational change often involves radically reconfiguring a complex network of people, tasks, and institutions that

Idea in Practice

Managing Your Environment

To minimize threats to eliminate you:

Operate in and above the fray.

Observe what's happening to your initiative, *as* it's happening. Frequently move back and forth from the dance floor to the balcony, asking, "What's really going on here?" "Who's defending old habits?"

Court the uncommitted.

The uncommitted but wary are crucial to your success. Show your intentions are serious, for example, by dismissing individuals who can't make required changes. And practice what you preach.

> **Example:** The editor of the *St. Petersburg Times* wanted to create a harder-hitting newspaper. He knew that

reporters—no longer sparing interviewees from warranted criticism—faced intense public pressure. He subjected *himself* to the same by insisting a story about his drunk-driving arrest appear on the paper's front page.

Cook the conflict.

Keep the heat high enough to motivate, but low enough to prevent explosions. *Raise the temperature* to make people confront hidden conflicts and other tough issues. Then *lower the heat* to reduce destructive turmoil. Slow the pace of change. Deliver humor, breaks, and images of a brighter future.

Place the work where it belongs.

Resist resolving conflicts yourself—people will blame *you* for whatever turmoil results. Mobilize *others* to solve problems.

have achieved a kind of modus vivendi, no matter how dysfunctional it appears to you. When the status quo is upset, people feel a sense of profound loss and dashed expectations. They may go through a period of feeling incompetent or disloyal. It's no wonder they resist the change or try to eliminate its visible agent. We offer here a number of techniques—relatively straightforward in concept but difficult to execute—for minimizing these external threats.

Operate in and above the fray

The ability to maintain perspective in the midst of action is critical to lowering resistance. Any military officer knows the importance of maintaining the capacity for reflection, especially in the "fog of

Example: When a star Chicago Bulls basketball player sat out a play, miffed because he wasn't tapped to take the game's final shot, the coach let the *team* handle the insubordination. An emotional conversation led by a team veteran reunited the players, who took the NBA series to a seventh game.

Managing Yourself

To avoid self-destructing during difficult change:

Restrain your desire for control and need for importance

Order for its own sake prevents organizations from handling contentious issues. And an inflated self-image fosters unhealthy dependence on you.

Example: Ken Olson, head of once-mighty Digital Equipment Corporation, encouraged such dependence that colleagues rarely challenged him. When he shunned the PC market (believing few people wanted PCs), top managers went along—initiating DEC's downfall.

Anchor yourself.

- Use a safe place (e.g., a friend's kitchen table) or routine (a daily walk) to repair psychological damage and recalibrate your moral compass.

- Acquire a confidant (*not* an ally from your organization) who supports you—not necessarily your initiative.

- Read attacks as reactions to your professional role, not to you personally. You'll remain calmer and keep people engaged.

war." Great athletes must simultaneously play the game and observe it as a whole. We call this skill "getting off the dance floor and going to the balcony," an image that captures the mental activity of stepping back from the action and asking, "What's really going on here?"

Leadership is an improvisational art. You may be guided by an overarching vision, clear values, and a strategic plan, but what you actually do from moment to moment cannot be scripted. You must respond as events unfold. To use our metaphor, you have to move back and forth from the balcony to the dance floor, over and over again throughout the days, weeks, months, and years. While today's plan may make sense now, tomorrow you'll discover the unanticipated effects of today's actions and have to adjust accordingly.

Sustaining good leadership, then, requires first and foremost the capacity to see what is happening to you and your initiative as it is happening and to understand how today's turns in the road will affect tomorrow's plans.

But taking a balcony perspective is extremely tough to do when you're fiercely engaged down below, being pushed and pulled by the events and people around you—and doing some pushing and pulling of your own. Even if you are able to break away, the practice of stepping back and seeing the big picture is complicated by several factors. For example, when you get some distance, you still must accurately interpret what you see and hear. This is easier said than done. In an attempt to avoid difficult change, people will naturally, even unconsciously, defend their habits and ways of thinking. As you seek input from a broad range of people, you'll constantly need to be aware of these hidden agendas. You'll also need to observe your own actions; seeing yourself objectively as you look down from the balcony is perhaps the hardest task of all.

Fortunately, you can learn to be both an observer and a participant at the same time. When you are sitting in a meeting, practice by watching what is happening while it is happening—even as you are part of what is happening. Observe the relationships and see how people's attention to one another can vary: supporting, thwarting, or listening. Watch people's body language. When you make a point, resist the instinct to stay perched on the edge of your seat, ready to defend what you said. A technique as simple as pushing your chair a few inches away from the table after you speak may provide the literal as well as metaphorical distance you need to become an observer.

Court the uncommitted

It's tempting to go it alone when leading a change initiative. There's no one to dilute your ideas or share the glory, and it's often just plain exciting. It's also foolish. You need to recruit partners, people who can help protect you from attacks and who can point out potentially fatal flaws in your strategy or initiative. Moreover, you are far less vulnerable when you are out on the point with a bunch of folks rather than alone. You also need to keep the opposition close. Knowing

Adaptive Versus Technical Change: Whose Problem Is It?

THE IMPORTANCE—AND DIFFICULTY—of distinguishing between adaptive and technical change can be illustrated with an analogy. When your car has problems, you go to a mechanic. Most of the time, the mechanic can fix the car. But if your car troubles stem from the way a family member drives, the problems are likely to recur. Treating the problems as purely technical ones—taking the car to the mechanic time and again to get it back on the road—masks the real issues. Maybe you need to get your mother to stop drinking and driving, get your grandfather to give up his driver's license, or get your teenager to be more cautious. Whatever the underlying problems, the mechanic can't solve them. Instead, changes in the family need to occur, and that won't be easy. People will resist the moves, even denying that such problems exist. That's because even those not directly affected by an adaptive change typically experience discomfort when someone upsets a group's or an organization's equilibrium.

Such resistance to adaptive change certainly happens in business. Indeed, it's the classic error: Companies treat adaptive challenges as if they were technical problems. For example, executives attempt to improve the bottom line by cutting costs across the board. Not only does this avoid the need to make tough choices about which areas should be trimmed, it also masks the fact that the company's real challenge lies in redesigning its strategy.

Treating adaptive challenges as technical ones permits executives to do what they have excelled at throughout their careers: solve other people's problems. And it allows others in the organization to enjoy the primordial peace of mind that comes from knowing that their commanding officer has a plan to maintain order and stability. After all, the executive doesn't have to instigate—and the people don't have to undergo—uncomfortable change. Most people would agree that, despite the selective pain of a cost-cutting exercise, it is less traumatic than reinventing a company.

what your opponents are thinking can help you challenge them more effectively and thwart their attempts to upset your agenda—or allow you to borrow ideas that will improve your initiative. Have coffee once a week with the person most dedicated to seeing you fail.

But while relationships with allies and opponents are essential, the people who will determine your success are often those in the middle, the uncommitted who nonetheless are wary of your plans.

They have no substantive stake in your initiative, but they do have a stake in the comfort, stability, and security of the status quo. They've seen change agents come and go, and they know that your initiative will disrupt their lives and make their futures uncertain. You want to be sure that this general uneasiness doesn't evolve into a move to push you aside.

These people will need to see that your intentions are serious—for example, that you are willing to let go of those who can't make the changes your initiative requires. But people must also see that you understand the loss you are asking them to accept. You need to name the loss, be it a change in time-honored work routines or an overhaul of the company's core values, and explicitly acknowledge the resulting pain. You might do this through a series of simple statements, but it often requires something more tangible and public—recall Franklin Roosevelt's radio "fireside chats" during the Great Depression—to convince people that you truly understand.

Beyond a willingness to accept casualties and acknowledge people's losses, two very personal types of action can defuse potential resistance to you and your initiatives. The first is practicing what you preach. In 1972, Gene Patterson took over as editor of the *St. Petersburg Times*. His mandate was to take the respected regional newspaper to a higher level, enhancing its reputation for fine writing while becoming a fearless and hard-hitting news source. This would require major changes not only in the way the community viewed the newspaper but also in the way *Times* reporters thought about themselves and their roles. Because prominent organizations and individuals would no longer be spared warranted criticism, reporters would sometimes be angrily rebuked by the subjects of articles.

Several years after Patterson arrived, he attended a party at the home of the paper's foreign editor. Driving home, he pulled up to a red light and scraped the car next to him. The police officer called to the scene charged Patterson with driving under the influence. Patterson phoned Bob Haiman, a veteran *Times* newsman who had just been appointed executive editor, and insisted that a story on his arrest be run. As Haiman recalls, he tried to talk Patterson out of it, arguing that DUI arrests that didn't involve injuries were rarely reported, even when prominent figures were involved. Patterson was adamant, however, and insisted that the story appear on page one.

Patterson, still viewed as somewhat of an outsider at the paper, knew that if he wanted his employees to follow the highest journalistic standards, he would have to display those standards, even when it hurt. Few leaders are called upon to disgrace themselves on the front page of a newspaper. But adopting the behavior you expect from others—whether it be taking a pay cut in tough times or spending a day working next to employees on a reconfigured production line—can be crucial in getting buy-in from people who might try to undermine your initiative.

The second thing you can do to neutralize potential opposition is to acknowledge your own responsibility for whatever problems the organization currently faces. If you have been with the company for some time, whether in a position of senior authority or not, you've likely contributed in some way to the current mess. Even if you are new, you need to identify areas of your own behavior that could stifle the change you hope to make.

In our teaching, training, and consulting, we often ask people to write or talk about a leadership challenge they currently face. Over the years, we have read and heard literally thousands of such challenges. Typically, in the first version of the story, the author is nowhere to be found. The underlying message: "If only other people would shape up, I could make progress here." But by too readily pointing your finger at others, you risk making yourself a target. Remember, you are asking people to move to a place where they are frightened to go. If at the same time you're blaming them for having to go there, they will undoubtedly turn against you.

In the early 1990s, Leslie Wexner, founder and CEO of the Limited, realized the need for major changes at the company, including a significant reduction in the workforce. But his consultant told him that something else had to change: long-standing habits that were at the heart of his self-image. In particular, he had to stop treating the company as if it were his family. The indulgent father had to become the chief personnel officer, putting the right people in the right jobs and holding them accountable for their work. "I was an athlete trained to be a baseball player," Wexner recalled during a recent speech at Harvard's Kennedy School. "And one day, someone tapped me on the shoulder and said, 'Football.' And I said, 'No, I'm a baseball player. 'And he said, 'Football.' And I said, 'I don't know how to play football. I'm not 6'4", and I don't weigh 300 pounds.' But if no one values baseball anymore, the baseball player will be out of business. So I looked into the mirror and said, 'Schlemiel, nobody wants to watch baseball. Make the transformation to football.'" His personal makeover—shedding the role of forgiving father to those widely viewed as not holding their own—helped sway other employees to back a corporate makeover. And his willingness to change helped protect him from attack during the company's long—and generally successful—turnaround period.

Cook the conflict

Managing conflict is one of the greatest challenges a leader of organizational change faces. The conflict may involve resistance to change, or it may involve clashing viewpoints about how the change should be carried out. Often, it will be latent rather than palpable. That's because most organizations are allergic to conflict, seeing it primarily as a source of danger, which it certainly can be. But conflict is a necessary part of the change process and, if handled properly, can serve as the engine of progress.

Thus, a key imperative for a leader trying to achieve significant change is to manage people's passionate differences in a way that diminishes their destructive potential and constructively harnesses their energy. Two techniques can help you achieve this. First, create a secure place where the conflicts can freely bubble up. Second, control the temperature to ensure that the conflict doesn't boil over—and burn you in the process.

The vessel in which a conflict is simmered—in which clashing points of view mix, lose some of their sharpness, and ideally blend into consensus—will look and feel quite different in different contexts. It may be a protected physical space, perhaps an off-site location where an outside facilitator helps a group work through its differences. It may be a clear set of rules and processes that give minority voices confidence that they will be heard without having to disrupt the proceedings to gain attention. It may be the shared language and history of an organization that binds people together through trying times. Whatever its form, it is a place or a means to contain the roiling forces unleashed by the threat of major change.

But a vessel can withstand only so much strain before it blows. A huge challenge you face as a leader is keeping your employees' stress at a productive level. The success of the change effort—as well as your own authority and even survival—requires you to monitor your organization's tolerance for heat and then regulate the temperature accordingly.

You first need to raise the heat enough that people sit up, pay attention, and deal with the real threats and challenges facing them. After all, without some distress, there's no incentive to change. You can constructively raise the temperature by focusing people's attention on the hard issues, by forcing them to take responsibility for tackling and solving those issues, and by bringing conflicts occurring behind closed doors out into the open.

But you have to lower the temperature when necessary to reduce what can be counterproductive turmoil. You can turn down the heat by slowing the pace of change or by tackling some relatively straightforward technical aspect of the problem, thereby reducing people's anxiety levels and allowing them to get warmed up for bigger challenges. You can provide structure to the problem-solving process, creating work groups with specific assignments, setting time parameters, establishing rules for decision making, and outlining reporting relationships. You can use humor or find an excuse for a break or a party to temporarily ease tensions. You can speak to people's fears and, more critically, to their hopes for a more promising future. By showing people how the future might look, you come to embody hope rather than fear, and you reduce the likelihood of becoming a lightning rod for the conflict.

The aim of both these tactics is to keep the heat high enough to motivate people but low enough to prevent a disastrous explosion— what we call a "productive range of distress." Remember, though, that most employees will reflexively want you to turn down the heat; their complaints may in fact indicate that the environment is just right for hard work to get done.

We've already mentioned a classic example of managing the distress of fundamental change: Franklin Roosevelt during the first few years of his presidency. When he took office in 1933, the chaos, tension, and anxiety brought on by the Depression ran extremely high. Demagogues stoked class, ethnic, and racial conflict that threatened to tear the nation apart. Individuals feared an uncertain future. So Roosevelt first did what he could to reduce the sense of disorder to a tolerable level. He took decisive and authoritative action—he pushed an extraordinary number of bills through Congress during his fabled first 100 days—and thereby gave Americans a sense of direction and safety, reassuring them that they were in capable hands. In his fireside chats, he spoke to people's anxiety and anger and laid out a positive vision for the future that made the stress of the current crisis bearable and seem a worthwhile price to pay for progress.

But he knew the problems facing the nation couldn't be solved from the White House. He needed to mobilize citizens and get them to dream up, try out, fight over, and ultimately own the sometimes painful solutions that would transform the country and move it forward. To do that, he needed to maintain a certain level of fermentation and distress. So, for example, he orchestrated conflicts over public priorities and programs among the large cast of creative people he brought into the government. By giving the same assignment to two different administrators and refusing to clearly define their roles, he got them to generate new and competing ideas. Roosevelt displayed both the acuity to recognize when the tension in the nation had risen too high and the emotional strength to take the heat and permit considerable anxiety to persist.

Place the work where it belongs

Because major change requires people across an entire organization to adapt, you as a leader need to resist the reflex reaction of providing people with the answers. Instead, force yourself to transfer, as Roosevelt did, much of the work and problem solving to others. If you don't, real and sustainable change won't occur. In addition, it's risky on a personal level to continue to hold on to the work that should be done by others.

As a successful executive, you have gained credibility and authority by demonstrating your capacity to solve other people's problems. This ability can be a virtue, until you find yourself faced with a situation in which you cannot deliver solutions. When this happens, all of your habits, pride, and sense of competence get thrown out of kilter because you must mobilize the work of others rather than find the way yourself. By trying to solve an adaptive challenge for people, at best you will reconfigure it as a technical problem and create some short-term relief. But the issue will not have gone away.

In the 1994 National Basketball Association Eastern Conference semifinals, the Chicago Bulls lost to the New York Knicks in the first two games of the best-of-seven series. Chicago was out to prove that it was more than just a one-man team, that it could win without Michael Jordan, who had retired at the end of the previous season.

In the third game, the score was tied at 102 with less than two seconds left. Chicago had the ball and a time-out to plan a final shot. Coach Phil Jackson called for Scottie Pippen, the Bulls' star since Jordan had retired, to make the inbound pass to Toni Kukoc for the final shot. As play was about to resume, Jackson noticed Pippen sitting at the far end of the bench. Jackson asked him whether he was in or out. "I'm out," said Pippen, miffed that he was not tapped to take the final shot. With only four players on the floor, Jackson quickly called another time-out and substituted an excellent passer, the reserve Pete Myers, for Pippen. Myers tossed a perfect pass to Kukoc, who spun around and sank a miraculous shot to win the game.

The Bulls made their way back to the locker room, their euphoria deflated by Pippen's extraordinary act of insubordination. Jackson recalls that as he entered a silent room, he was uncertain about what to do. Should he punish Pippen? Make him apologize? Pretend the whole thing never happened? All eyes were on him. The coach looked around, meeting the gaze of each player, and said, "What happened has hurt us. Now you have to work this out."

Jackson knew that if he took action to resolve the immediate crisis, he would have made Pippen's behavior a matter between coach and player. But he understood that a deeper issue was at the heart of the incident: Who were the Chicago Bulls without Michael Jordan? It wasn't about who was going to succeed Jordan, because no one was; it was about whether the players could jell as a team where no one person dominated and every player was willing to do whatever it took to help. The issue rested with the players, not him, and only they could resolve it. It did not matter what they decided at that moment; what mattered was that they, not Jackson, did the deciding. What followed was a discussion led by an emotional Bill Cartwright, a team veteran. According to Jackson, the conversation brought the team closer together. The Bulls took the series to a seventh game before succumbing to the Knicks.

Jackson gave the work of addressing both the Pippen and the Jordan issues back to the team for another reason: If he had taken ownership of the problem, he would have become the issue, at least for the moment. In his case, his position as coach probably wouldn't have been threatened. But in other situations, taking responsibility for resolving a conflict within the organization poses risks. You are likely to find yourself resented by the faction that you decide against and held responsible by nearly everyone for the turmoil your decision generates. In the eyes of many, the only way to neutralize the threat is to get rid of you.

Despite that risk, most executives can't resist the temptation to solve fundamental organizational problems by themselves. People expect you to get right in there and fix things, to take a stand and resolve the problem. After all, that is what top managers are paid to do. When you fulfill those expectations, people will call you admirable and courageous—even a "leader"—and that is flattering. But challenging your employees' expectations requires greater courage and leadership.

The Dangers Within

We have described a handful of leadership tactics you can use to interact with the people around you, particularly those who might undermine your initiatives. Those tactics can help advance your initiatives and, just as important, ensure that you remain in a position where you can bring them to fruition. But from our own observations and painful personal experiences, we know that one of the surest ways for an organization to bring you down is simply to let you precipitate your own demise.

In the heat of leadership, with the adrenaline pumping, it is easy to convince yourself that you are not subject to the normal human frailties that can defeat ordinary mortals. You begin to act as if you are indestructible. But the intellectual, physical, and emotional challenges of leadership are fierce. So, in addition to getting on the balcony, you need to regularly step into the inner chamber of your being and assess the tolls those challenges are taking. If you don't, your seemingly indestructible self can self-destruct. This, by the way, is an ideal outcome for your foes—and even friends who oppose your initiative—because no one has to feel responsible for your downfall.

Manage your hungers

We all have hungers, expressions of our normal human needs. But sometimes those hungers disrupt our capacity to act wisely or purposefully. Whether inherited or products of our upbringing, some of these hungers may be so strong that they render us constantly vulnerable. More typically, a stressful situation or setting can exaggerate a normal level of need, amplifying our desires and overwhelming our usual self-discipline. Two of the most common and dangerous hungers are the desire for control and the desire for importance.

Everyone wants to have some measure of control over his or her life. Yet some people's need for control is disproportionately high. They might have grown up in a household that was either tightly structured or unusually chaotic; in either case, the situation drove them to become masters at taming chaos not only in their own lives but also in their organizations.

That need for control can be a source of vulnerability. Initially, of course, the ability to turn disorder into order may be seen as an attribute. In an organization facing turmoil, you may seem like a godsend if you are able (and desperately want) to step in and take charge. By lowering the distress to a tolerable level, you keep the kettle from boiling over.

But in your desire for order, you can mistake the means for the end. Rather than ensuring that the distress level in an organization remains high enough to mobilize progress on the issues, you focus on maintaining order as an end in itself. Forcing people to make the difficult trade-offs required by fundamental change threatens a return to the disorder you loathe. Your ability to bring the situation under control also suits the people in the organization, who naturally prefer calm to chaos. Unfortunately, this desire for control makes you vulnerable to, and an agent of, the organization's wish to avoid working through contentious issues. While this may ensure your survival in the short term, ultimately you may find yourself accused, justifiably, of failing to deal with the tough challenges when there was still time to do so.

Most people also have some need to feel important and affirmed by others. The danger here is that you will let this affirmation give you an inflated view of yourself and your cause. A grandiose sense of self-importance often leads to self-deception. In particular, you tend to forget the creative role that doubt—which reveals parts of reality that you wouldn't otherwise see—plays in getting your organization to improve. The absence of doubt leads you to see only that which confirms your own competence, which will virtually guarantee disastrous missteps.

Another harmful side effect of an inflated sense of self-importance is that you will encourage people in the organization to become dependent on you. The higher the level of distress, the greater their hopes and expectations that you will provide deliverance. This relieves them of any responsibility for moving the organization forward. But their dependence can be detrimental not only to the group but to you personally. Dependence can quickly turn to contempt as your constituents discover your human shortcomings.

Two well-known stories from the computer industry illustrate the perils of dependency—and how to avoid them. Ken Olsen, the founder of Digital Equipment Corporation, built the company into a 120,000-person operation that, at its peak, was the chief rival of IBM.

A generous man, he treated his employees extraordinarily well and experimented with personnel policies designed to increase the creativity, teamwork, and satisfaction of his workforce. This, in tandem with the company's success over the years, led the company's top management to turn to him as the sole decision maker on all key issues. His decision to shun the personal computer market because of his belief that few people would ever want to own a PC, which seemed reasonable at the time, is generally viewed as the beginning of the end for the company. But that isn't the point; everyone in business makes bad decisions. The point is, Olsen had fostered such an atmosphere of dependence that his decisions were rarely challenged by colleagues—at least not until it was too late.

Contrast that decision with Bill Gates's decision some years later to keep Microsoft out of the Internet business. It didn't take long for him to reverse his stand and launch a corporate overhaul that had Microsoft's delivery of Internet services as its centerpiece. After watching the rapidly changing computer industry and listening carefully to colleagues, Gates changed his mind with no permanent damage to his sense of pride and an enhanced reputation due to his nimble change of course.

Anchor yourself

To survive the turbulent seas of a change initiative, you need to find ways to steady and stabilize yourself. First, you must establish a safe harbor where each day you can reflect on the previous day's journey, repair the psychological damage you have incurred, renew your stores of emotional resources, and recalibrate your moral compass. Your haven might be a physical place, such as the kitchen table of a friend's house, or a regular routine, such as a daily walk through the neighborhood. Whatever the sanctuary, you need to use and protect it. Unfortunately, seeking such respite is often seen as a luxury, making it one of the first things to go when life gets stressful and you become pressed for time.

Second, you need a confidant, someone you can talk to about what's in your heart and on your mind without fear of being judged or betrayed. Once the undigested mess is on the table, you can begin to separate, with your confidant's honest input, what is worthwhile from what is simply venting. The confidant, typically not a coworker, can also pump you up when you're down and pull you back to earth when you start taking praise too seriously. But don't confuse confidants with allies: Instead of supporting your current initiative, a confidant simply supports you. A common mistake is to seek a confidant among trusted allies, whose personal loyalty may evaporate when a new issue more important to them than you begins to emerge and take center stage.

Perhaps most important, you need to distinguish between your personal self, which can serve as an anchor in stormy weather, and your professional role, which never will. It is easy to mix up the two. And other people only increase the confusion: Colleagues, subordinates, and even bosses often act as if the role you play is the real you. But that is not the case, no matter how much of yourself—your passions, your values, your talents—you genuinely and laudably pour into your professional role. Ask anyone who has experienced the rude awakening that comes when they leave a position of authority and suddenly find that their phone calls aren't returned as quickly as they used to be.

That harsh lesson holds another important truth that is easily forgotten: When people attack someone in a position of authority, more often than not they are attacking the role, not the person. Even when attacks on you are highly personal, you need to read them primarily as reactions to how you, in your role, are affecting people's lives. Understanding the criticism for what it is prevents it from undermining your stability and sense of self-worth. And that's important because when you feel the sting of an attack, you are likely to become defensive and lash out at your critics, which can precipitate your downfall.

We hasten to add that criticism may contain legitimate points about how you are performing your role. For example, you may have been tactless in raising an issue with your organization, or you may have turned the heat up too quickly on a change initiative. But, at its heart, the criticism is usually about the issue, not you. Through the guise of attacking you personally, people often are simply trying to neutralize the threat they perceive in your point of view. Does anyone ever attack you when you hand out big checks or deliver good news? People attack your personality, style, or judgment when they don't like the message.

When you take "personal" attacks personally, you unwittingly conspire in one of the common ways you can be taken out of action—you make yourself the issue. Contrast the manner in which presidential candidates Gary Hart and Bill Clinton handled charges of philandering. Hart angrily counterattacked, criticizing the scruples of the reporters who had shadowed him. This defensive personal response kept the focus on his behavior. Clinton, on national television, essentially admitted he had strayed, acknowledging his piece of the mess. His strategic handling of the situation allowed him to return the campaign's focus to policy issues. Though both attacks were extremely personal, only Clinton understood that they were basically attacks on positions he represented and the role he was seeking to play.

Do not underestimate the difficulty of distinguishing self from role and responding coolly to what feels like a personal attack—particularly when the criticism comes, as it will, from people you care about. But disciplining yourself to do so can provide you with an anchor that will keep you from running aground and give you the stability to remain calm, focused, and persistent in engaging people with the tough issues.

Why Lead?

We will have failed if this "survival manual" for avoiding the perils of leadership causes you to become cynical or callous in your leadership effort or to shun the challenges of leadership altogether. We haven't touched on the thrill of inspiring people to come up with creative solutions that can transform an organization for the better. We hope we have shown that the essence of leadership lies in the capacity to deliver disturbing news and raise difficult questions in a way that moves people to take up the message rather than kill the messenger. But we haven't talked about the reasons that someone might want to take these risks.

Of course, many people who strive for high-authority positions are attracted to power. But in the end, that isn't enough to make the high stakes of the game worthwhile. We would argue that, when they look deep within themselves, people grapple with the challenges of leadership in order to make a positive difference in the lives of others.

When corporate presidents and vice presidents reach their late fifties, they often look back on careers devoted to winning in the marketplace. They may have succeeded remarkably, yet some people have difficulty making sense of their lives in light of what they have given up. For too many, their accomplishments seem empty. They question whether they should have been more aggressive in questioning corporate purposes or creating more ambitious visions for their companies.

Our underlying assumption in this article is that you can lead *and* stay alive—not just register a pulse, but really be alive. But the classic protective devices of a person in authority tend to insulate them from those qualities that foster an acute experience of living. Cynicism, often dressed up as realism, undermines creativity and daring. Arrogance, often posing as authoritative knowledge, snuffs out curiosity and the eagerness to question. Callousness, sometimes portrayed as the thick skin of experience, shuts out compassion for others.

The hard truth is that it is not possible to know the rewards and joys of leadership without experiencing the pain as well. But staying in the game and bearing that pain is worth it, not only for the positive changes you can make in the lives of others but also for the meaning it gives your own.

Originally published in June 2002. Reprint R0206C

The Real Reason People Won't Change

by Robert Kegan and Lisa Laskow Lahey

EVERY MANAGER IS FAMILIAR with the employee who just won't change. Sometimes it's easy to see why—the employee fears a shift in power, the need to learn new skills, the stress of having to join a new team. In other cases, such resistance is far more puzzling. An employee has the skills and smarts to make a change with ease, has shown a deep commitment to the company, genuinely supports the change—and yet, inexplicably, does nothing.

What's going on? As organizational psychologists, we have seen this dynamic literally hundreds of times, and our research and analysis have recently led us to a surprising yet deceptively simple conclusion. Resistance to change does not reflect opposition, nor is it merely a result of inertia. Instead, even as they hold a sincere commitment to change, many people are unwittingly applying productive energy toward a hidden *competing commitment*. The resulting dynamic equilibrium stalls the effort in what looks like resistance but is in fact a kind of personal immunity to change.

When you, as a manager, uncover an employee's competing commitment, behavior that has seemed irrational and ineffective suddenly becomes stunningly sensible and masterful—but unfortunately, on behalf of a goal that conflicts with what you and even the employee are trying to achieve. You find out that the project leader who's dragging his feet has an unrecognized competing commitment to avoid the even tougher assignment—one he fears he can't handle—that might come his way next if he delivers too successfully on the task at hand. Or you find that the person who won't collaborate despite a passionate and sincere commitment to teamwork is equally dedicated to avoiding the conflict that naturally attends any ambitious team activity.

In these pages, we'll look at competing commitments in detail and take you through a process to help your employees overcome their immunity to change. The process may sound straightforward, but it is by no means quick or easy. On the contrary, it challenges the very psychological foundations upon which people function. It asks people to call into question beliefs they've long held close, perhaps since childhood. And it requires people to admit to painful, even embarrassing, feelings that they would not ordinarily disclose to others or even to themselves. Indeed, some people will opt not to disrupt their immunity to change, choosing instead to continue their fruitless struggle against their competing commitments.

As a manager, you must guide people through this exercise with understanding and sensitivity. If your employees are to engage in honest introspection and candid disclosure, they must understand that their revelations won't be used against them. The goal of this exploration is solely to help them become more effective, not to find flaws in their work or character. As you support your employees in unearthing and challenging their innermost assumptions, you may at times feel you're playing the role of a psychologist. But in a sense, managers *are* psychologists. After all, helping people overcome their limitations to become more successful at work is at the very heart of effective management.

We'll describe this delicate process in detail, but first let's look at some examples of competing commitments in action.

Shoveling Sand Against the Tide

Competing commitments cause valued employees to behave in ways that seem inexplicable and irremediable, and this is enormously

Idea in Brief

Tearing out your managerial hair over employees who just won't change—especially the ones who are clearly smart, skilled, and deeply committed to your company and your plans for improvement?

Before you throw up your hands in frustration, listen to recent psychological research: These otherwise valued employees aren't *purposefully* subversive or resistant. Instead, they may be unwittingly caught in a **competing commitment** —a subconscious, hidden goal that conflicts with their *stated* commitments. For example: A project leader dragging his feet has an unrecognized competing commitment to avoid tougher assignments that may come his way if he delivers too successfully on the current project.

Competing commitments make people personally immune to change. Worse, they can undermine your best employees'—and your company's—success.

If the thought of tackling these hidden commitments strikes you as a psychological quagmire, you're not alone. However, you can help employees uncover and move beyond their competing commitments—*without* having to "put them on the couch." But take care: You'll be challenging employees' deepest psychological foundations and questioning their longest-held beliefs.

Why bother, you ask? Consider the rewards: You help talented employees become much more effective and make far more significant contributions to your company. And, you discover what's *really* going on when people who seem genuinely committed to change dig in their heels.

frustrating to managers. Take the case of John, a talented manager at a software company. (Like all examples in this article, John's experiences are real, although we have altered identifying features. In some cases, we've constructed composite examples.) John was a big believer in open communication and valued close working relationships, yet his caustic sense of humor consistently kept colleagues at a distance. And though he wanted to move up in the organization, his personal style was holding him back. Repeatedly, John was counseled on his behavior, and he readily agreed that he needed to change the way he interacted with others in the organization. But time after

Idea in Practice

Use these steps to break through an employee's immunity to change:

Diagnose the Competing Commitment

Take two to three hours to explore these questions with the employee:

"What would you like to see changed at work, so you could be more effective, or so work would be more satisfying?" Responses are usually complaints—e.g., Tom, a manager, grumbled, "My subordinates keep me out of the loop."

"What commitment does your complaint imply?" Complaints indicate what people care about most—e.g., Tom revealed, "I believe in open, candid communication."

"What are *you* doing, or not doing, to keep your commitment from being more fully realized?" Tom admitted, "When people bring bad news, I tend to shoot the messenger."

"Imagine doing the *opposite* of the undermining behavior. Do you feel any discomfort, worry, or vague fear?" Tom imagined listening calmly and openly to bad news and concluded, "I'm afraid I'll hear about a problem I can't fix."

"By engaging in this undermining behavior, what worrisome outcome are you committed to preventing?" The answer *is* the competing commitment—what causes them to dig in their heels against change. Tom conceded, *"I'm committed to not learning about problems I can't fix."*

Identify the Big Assumption

This is the worldview that colors everything we see and that generates our competing commitment.

People often form big assumptions early in life and then seldom, if

time, he reverted to his old patterns. Why, his boss wondered, did John continue to undermine his own advancement?

As it happened, John was a person of color working as part of an otherwise all-white executive team. When he went through an exercise designed to help him unearth his competing commitments, he made a surprising discovery about himself. Underneath it all, John believed that if he became too well integrated with the team, it would threaten his sense of loyalty to his own racial group. Moving too close to the mainstream made him feel very uncomfortable, as if he were ever, examine them. They're woven into the very fabric of our lives. But only by bringing them into the light can people finally challenge their deepest beliefs and recognize why they're engaging in seemingly contradictory behavior.

To identify the big assumption, guide an employee through this exercise:

Create a sentence stem that inverts the competing commitment, then "fill in the blank." Tom turned his competing commitment to not hearing about problems he couldn't fix into this big assumption: "I assume that if I *did* hear about problems I can't fix, *people would discover I'm not qualified to do the job.*"

Test—and Consider Replacing— the Big Assumption

By analyzing the circumstances leading up to and reinforcing their big assumptions, employees empower themselves to test those assumptions. They can now carefully and safely experiment with behaving differently than they usually do.

After running several such tests, employees may feel ready to reevaluate the big assumption itself—and possibly even replace it with a new worldview that more accurately reflects their abilities.

At the very least, they'll eventually find more effective ways to support their competing commitment *without* sabotaging other commitments. *They* achieve ever-greater accomplishments—and your *organization* benefits by finally gaining greater access to their talents.

becoming "one of them" and betraying his family and friends. So when people gathered around his ideas and suggestions, he'd tear down their support with sarcasm, inevitably (and effectively) returning himself to the margins, where he was more at ease. In short, while John was genuinely committed to working well with his colleagues, he had an equally powerful competing commitment to keeping his distance.

Consider, too, a manager we'll call Helen, a rising star at a large manufacturing company. Helen had been assigned responsibility for speeding up production of the company's most popular product, yet

Getting Groups to Change

ALTHOUGH COMPETING COMMITMENTS and big assumptions tend to be deeply personal, groups are just as susceptible as individuals to the dynamics of immunity to change. Face-to-face teams, departments, and even companies as a whole can fall prey to inner contradictions that "protect" them from significant changes they may genuinely strive for. The leadership team of a video production company, for instance, enjoyed a highly collaborative, largely flat organizational structure. A year before we met the group, team members had undertaken a planning process that led them to a commitment of which they were unanimously in favor: In order to ensure that the company would grow in the way the team wished, each of the principals would take responsibility for aggressively overseeing a distinct market segment.

The members of the leadership team told us they came out of this process with a great deal of momentum. They knew which markets to target, they had formed some concrete plans for moving forward, and they had clearly assigned accountability for each market. Yet a year later, the group had to admit it had accomplished very little, despite the enthusiasm. There were lots of rational explanations: "We were unrealistic; we thought we could do new things and still have time to keep meeting our present obligations." "We didn't pursue new clients aggressively enough." "We tried new things but gave up too quickly if they didn't immediately pay off."

Efforts to overcome these barriers—to pursue clients more aggressively, for instance—didn't work because they didn't get to the cause of the unproductive behavior. But by seeing the team's explanations as a potential window

she was spinning her wheels. When her boss, Andrew, realized that an important deadline was only two months away and she hadn't filed a single progress report, he called her into a meeting to discuss the project. Helen agreed that she was far behind schedule, acknowledging that she had been stalling in pulling together the team. But at the same time she showed a genuine commitment to making the project a success. The two developed a detailed plan for changing direction, and Andrew assumed the problem was resolved. But three weeks after the meeting, Helen still hadn't launched the team.

Why was Helen unable to change her behavior? After intense self-examination in a workshop with several of her colleagues, she came to an unexpected conclusion: Although she truly wanted the project to succeed, she had an accompanying, unacknowledged commitment into the bigger competing commitment, we were able to help the group better understand its predicament. We asked, "Can you identify even the vaguest fear or worry about what might happen if you *did* more aggressively pursue the new markets? Or if you reduced some of your present activity on behalf of building the new business?" Before long, a different discourse began to emerge, and the other half of a striking groupwide contradiction came into view: The principals were worried that pursuing the plan would drive them apart functionally and emotionally.

"We now realize we are also committed to preserving the noncompetitive, intellectually rewarding, and cocreative spirit of our corporate enterprise," they concluded. On behalf of this commitment, the team members had to commend themselves on how "noncompetitively" and "cocreatively" they were finding ways to undermine the strategic plans they still believed were the best route to the company's future success. The team's big assumptions? "We assumed that pursuing the target-market strategy, with each of us taking aggressive responsibility for a given segment, would create the 'silos' we have long happily avoided and would leave us more isolated from one another. We also assumed the strategy would make us more competitively disposed toward one another." Whether or not the assumptions were true, they would have continued to block the group's efforts until they were brought to light. In fact, as the group came to discover, there were a variety of moves that would allow the leadership team to preserve a genuinely collaborative collegiality while pursuing the new corporate strategy.

to maintaining a subordinate position in relation to Andrew. At a deep level, Helen was concerned that if she succeeded in her new role—one she was excited about and eager to undertake—she would become more a peer than a subordinate. She was uncertain whether Andrew was prepared for the turn their relationship would take. Worse, a promotion would mean that she, not Andrew, would be ultimately accountable for the results of her work—and Helen feared she wouldn't be up to the task.

These stories shed some light on the nature of immunity to change. The inconsistencies between John's and Helen's stated goals and their actions reflect neither hypocrisy nor unspoken reluctance to change but the paralyzing effect of competing commitments. Any manager who seeks to help John communicate more effectively or

Helen move her project forward, without understanding that each is also struggling unconsciously toward an opposing agenda, is shoveling sand against the tide.

Diagnosing Immunity to Change

Competing commitments aren't distressing only to the boss; they're frustrating to employees as well. People with the most

---

A diagnostic test for immunity to change

The most important steps in diagnosing immunity to change are uncovering employees' competing commitments and unearthing their big assumptions. To do so, we ask a series of questions and record key responses in a simple grid. Below we've listed the responses for six people who went through this exercise, including the examples described in the text. The grid paints a picture of the change-immunity system, making sense of a previously puzzling dynamic.

	Stated commitment I am committed to . . .	What am I doing, or not doing, that is keeping my stated commitment from being fully realized?	Competing commitments	Big assumptions
John	. . .high quality communication with my colleagues.	Sometimes I use sarcastic humor to get my point across.	I am committed to maintaining a distance from my white colleagues.	I assume I will lose my authentic connection to my racial group if I get too integrated into the mainstream.
Helen	. . .the new initiative.	I don't push for top performance from my team members or myself; I accept mediocre products and thinking too often; I don't prioritize.	I am committed to not upsetting my relationship with my boss by leaving the mentee role.	I assume my boss will stop supporting me if I move toward becoming his peer; I assume that I don't have what it takes to successfully carry out a cutting-edge project.

Tom	...hearing from my subordinates and maximizing the flow of information into my office.	I don't ask questions or ask to be kept in the loop on sensitive or delicate matters; I shoot the messenger when I hear bad news.	I am committed to not learning about things I can't do anything about.	I assume as a leader I should be able to address all problems; I assume I will be seen as incompetent if I can't solve all problems that come up.
Mary	...distributed leadership by enabling people to make decisions.	I don't delegate enough; I don't pass on the necessary information to the people I distribute leadership to.	I am committed to having things go my way, to being in control, and to ensuring that the work is done to my high standards.	I assume that other people will waste my time and theirs if I don't step in; I assume others aren't as smart as I am.
Bill	...being a team player.	I don't collaborate enough; I make unilateral decisions too often; I don't really take people's input into account.	I am committed to being the one who gets the credit and to avoiding the frustration or conflict that comes with collaboration.	I assume that no one will appreciate me if I am not seen as the source of success; I assume nothing good will come of my being frustrated or in conflict.
Jane	...turning around my department.	Too often I let things slide; I'm not proactive enough in getting people to follow through with their tasks.	I am committed to not setting full sail until I have a clear map of how we get our department from here to there.	I assume that if I take my group out into deep waters and discover I am unable to get us to the other side, I will be seen as an incompetent leader who is undeserving of trust or responsibility.

sincere intentions often unwittingly create for themselves Sisyphean tasks. And they are almost always tremendously relieved when they discover just why they feel as if they are rolling a boulder up a hill only to have it roll back down again. Even though uncovering a competing commitment can open up a host of new concerns, the discovery offers hope for finally accomplishing the primary, stated commitment.

Based on the past 15 years of working with hundreds of managers in a variety of companies, we've developed a three-stage process to help organizations figure out what's getting in the way of change. First, managers guide employees through a set of questions designed to uncover competing commitments. Next, employees examine these commitments to determine the underlying assumptions at their core. And finally, employees start the process of changing their behavior.

We'll walk through the process fairly quickly below, but it's important to note that each step will take time. Just uncovering the competing commitment will require at least two or three hours, because people need to reflect on each question and the implications of their answers. The process of challenging competing commitments and making real progress toward overcoming immunity to change unfolds over a longer period—weeks or even months. But just getting the commitments on the table can have a noticeable effect on the decisions people make and the actions they take.

Uncovering Competing Commitments

Overcoming immunity to change starts with uncovering competing commitments. In our work, we've found that even though people keep their competing commitments well hidden, you can draw them out by asking a series of questions—as long as the employees believe that personal and potentially embarrassing disclosures won't be used inappropriately. It can be very powerful to guide people through this diagnostic exercise in a group—typically with several volunteers making their own discoveries public—so people can see that others, even the company's star performers, have competing commitments and inner contradictions of their own.

The first question we ask is, *What would you like to see changed at work, so that you could be more effective or so that work would be more satisfying?* Responses to this question are nearly always couched in a complaint—a form of communication that most managers bemoan because of its negative, unproductive tone. But complaints can be immensely useful. People complain only about the things they care about, and they complain the loudest about the things they care about most. With little effort, people can turn their familiar, uninspiring gripes into something that's more likely to energize and motivate them—a commitment, genuinely their own.

To get there, you need to ask a second question: *What commitments does your complaint imply?* A project leader we worked with, we'll call him Tom, had grumbled, "My subordinates keep me out of the loop on important developments in my project." This complaint yielded the statement, "I believe in open and candid communication." A line manager we'll call Mary lamented people's unwillingness to speak up at meetings; her complaint implied a commitment to shared decision making.

While undoubtedly sincere in voicing such commitments, people can nearly always identify some way in which they are in part responsible for preventing them from being fulfilled. Thus, the third question is: *What are you doing, or not doing, that is keeping your commitment from being more fully realized?* Invariably, in our experience, people can identify these undermining behaviors in just a couple of seconds. For example, Tom admitted: "When people bring me bad news, I tend to shoot the messenger." And Mary acknowledged that she didn't delegate much and that she sometimes didn't release all the information people needed in order to make good decisions.

In both cases, there may well have been other circumstances contributing to the shortfalls, but clearly both Tom and Mary were engaging in behavior that was affecting the people around them. Most people recognize this about themselves right away and are quick to say, "I need to stop doing that." Indeed, Tom had repeatedly vowed to listen more openly to potential problems that would slow his projects. However, the purpose of this exercise is not to make these behaviors disappear—at least not now. The purpose is to understand why people behave in ways that undermine their own success.

The next step, then, is to invite people to consider the consequences of forgoing the behavior. We do this by asking a fourth question: *If you imagine doing the opposite of the undermining behavior, do you detect in yourself any discomfort, worry, or vague fear?* Tom imagined himself listening calmly and openly to some bad news about a project and concluded, "I'm afraid I'll hear about a problem that I can't fix, something that I can't do anything about." And Mary? She considered allowing people more latitude and realized that, quite frankly, she feared people wouldn't make good decisions and she would be forced to carry out a strategy she thought would lead to an inferior result.

The final step is to transform that passive fear into a statement that reflects an active commitment to preventing certain outcomes. We ask, *By engaging in this undermining behavior, what worrisome outcome are you committed to preventing?* The resulting answer is the competing commitment, which lies at the very heart of a person's immunity to change. Tom admitted, "I am committed to not learning about problems I can't fix." By intimidating his staff, he prevented them from delivering bad news, protecting himself from the fear that he was not in control of the project. Mary, too, was protecting herself—in her case, against the consequences of bad decisions. "I am committed to making sure my group does not make decisions that I don't like."

Such revelations can feel embarrassing. While primary commitments nearly always reflect noble goals that people would be happy to shout from the rooftops, competing commitments are very personal, reflecting vulnerabilities that people fear will undermine how they are regarded both by others and themselves. Little wonder people keep them hidden and hasten to cover them up again once they're on the table.

But competing commitments should not be seen as weaknesses. They represent some version of self-protection, a perfectly natural and reasonable human impulse. The question is, if competing commitments are a form of self-protection, what are people protecting themselves from? The answers usually lie in what we call their *big assumptions*—deeply rooted beliefs about themselves and the world around them. These assumptions put an order to the world and at the same time suggest ways in which the world can go out of order. Competing commitments arise from these assumptions, driving behaviors unwittingly designed to keep the picture intact.

Examining the Big Assumption

People rarely realize they hold big assumptions because, quite simply, they accept them as reality. Often formed long ago and seldom, if ever, critically examined, big assumptions are woven into the very fabric of people's existence. (For more on the grip that big assumptions hold on people, see the sidebar "Big Assumptions: How Our Perceptions Shape Our Reality.") But with a little help, most people can call them up fairly easily, especially once they've identified their competing commitments. To do this, we first ask people to create the beginning of a sentence by inverting the competing commitment, and then we ask them to fill in the blank. For Tom ("I am committed to not hearing about problems I can't fix"), the big assumption turned out to be, "I assume that if I *did* hear about problems I can't fix, people would discover I'm not qualified to do my job." Mary's big assumption was that her teammates weren't as smart or experienced as she and that she'd be wasting her time and others' if she didn't maintain control. Returning to our earlier story, John's big assumption might be, "I assume that if I develop unambivalent relationships with my white coworkers, I will sacrifice my racial identity and alienate my own community."

This is a difficult process, and it doesn't happen all at once, because admitting to big assumptions makes people uncomfortable. The process can put names to very personal feelings people are reluctant to disclose, such as deep-seated fears or insecurities, highly discouraging or simplistic views of human nature, or perceptions of their own superior abilities or intellect. Unquestioning acceptance of a big assumption anchors and sustains an immune system: A competing commitment makes all the sense in the world, and the person continues to engage in behaviors that support it, albeit unconsciously, to the detriment of his or her "official," stated commitment. Only by bringing big assumptions to light can people

Big Assumptions: How Our Perceptions Shape Our Reality

BIG ASSUMPTIONS REFLECT the very human manner in which we invent or shape a picture of the world and then take our inventions for reality. This is easiest to see in children. The delight we take in their charming distortions is a kind of celebration that they are actively making sense of the world, even if a bit eccentrically. As one story goes, two youngsters had been learning about Hindu culture and were taken with a representation of the universe in which the world sits atop a giant elephant, and the elephant sits atop an even more giant turtle. "I wonder what the turtle sits on," says one of the children. "I think from then on," says the other, "it's turtles all the way down."

But deep within our amusement may lurk a note of condescension, an implication that this is what distinguishes children from grown-ups. Their meaning-making is subject to youthful distortions, we assume. Ours represents an accurate map of reality.

But does it? Are we really finished discovering, once we have reached adulthood, that our maps don't match the territory? The answer is clearly no. In our 20 years of longitudinal and cross-sectional research, we've discovered that adults must grow into and out of several qualitatively different views of

finally challenge their assumptions and recognize why they are engaging in seemingly contradictory behavior.

Questioning the Big Assumption

Once people have identified their competing commitments and the big assumptions that sustain them, most are prepared to take some immediate action to overcome their immunity. But the first part of the process involves observation, not action, which can be frustrating for high achievers accustomed to leaping into motion to solve problems. Let's take a look at the steps in more detail.

Step 1: Notice and record current behavior
Employees must first take notice of what does and doesn't happen as a consequence of holding big assumptions to be true. We specifically ask people *not* to try to make any changes in their thinking or

the world if they are to master the challenges of their life experiences (see Robert Kegan, *In Over Our Heads,* Harvard University Press, 1994).

A woman we met from Australia told us about her experience living in the United States for a year. "Not only do you drive on the wrong side of the street over here," she said, "your steering wheels are on the wrong side, too. I would routinely pile into the right side of the car to drive off, only to discover I needed to get out and walk over to the other side.

"One day," she continued, "I was thinking about six different things, and I got into the right side of the car, took out my keys, and was prepared to drive off. I looked up and thought to myself, 'My God, here in the violent and lawless United States, they are even stealing *steering wheels!* '"

Of course, the countervailing evidence was just an arm's length to her left, but—and this is the main point—*why should she look?* Our big assumptions create a disarming and deluding sense of certainty. If we know where a steering wheel belongs, we are unlikely to look for it some place else. If we know what our company, department, boss, or subordinate can and can't do, why should we look for countervailing data—even if it is just an arm's length away?

---

behavior at this time but just to become more aware of their actions in relation to their big assumptions. This gives people the opportunity to develop a better appreciation for how and in what contexts big assumptions influence their lives. John, for example, who had assumed that working well with his white colleagues would estrange him from his ethnic group, saw that he had missed an opportunity to get involved in an exciting, high-profile initiative because he had mocked the idea when it first came up in a meeting.

Step 2: Look for contrary evidence
Next, employees must look actively for experiences that might cast doubt on the validity of their big assumptions. Because big assumptions are held as fact, they actually inform what people see, leading them to systematically (but unconsciously) attend to certain data and avoid or ignore other data. By asking people to search specifically for experiences that would cause them to question their

assumptions, we help them see that they have filtering out certain types of information—information that could weaken the grip of the big assumptions.

When John looked around him, he considered for the first time that an African-American manager in another department had strong working relationships with her mostly white colleagues, yet seemed not to have compromised her personal identity. He also had to admit that when he had been thrown onto an urgent task force the year before, he had worked many hours alongside his white colleagues and found the experience satisfying; he had felt of his usual ambivalence.

Step 3: Explore the history

In this step, we people to become the "biographers" of their assumptions: How and when did the assumptions first take hold? How long have they been around? What have been some of their critical turning points?

Typically, this step leads people to earlier life experiences, almost always to times before their current jobs and relationships with current coworkers. This reflection usually makes people dissatisfied with the foundations of their big assumptions, especially when they see that these have accompanied them to their current positions and have been coloring their experiences for many years. Recently, a CEO expressed astonishment as she realized she'd been applying the same self-protective stance in her work that she'd developed during a difficult divorce years before. Just as commonly, as was the case for John, people trace their big assumptions to early experiences with parents, siblings, or friends. Understanding the circumstances that influenced the formation of the assumptions can free people to consider whether these beliefs apply to their present selves.

Step 4: Test the assumption

This step entails creating and running a modest test of the big assumption. This is the first time we ask people to consider making changes in their behavior. Each employee should come up with a scenario and run it by a partner who serves as a sounding board.

(Left to their own devices, people tend to create tests that are either too risky or so tentative that they don't actually challenge the assumption and in fact reaf-firm its validity.) After conferring with a partner, John, for instance, volunteered to join a short-term committee looking at his department's process for evaluating new product ideas. Because the team would dissolve after a month, he would be able to extricate himself fairly quickly if he grew too uncomfortable with the relationships. But the experience would force him to spend a significant amount of time with several of his white colleagues during that month and would provide him an opportunity to test his sense of the real costs of being a full team member.

Step 5: Evaluate the results
In the last step, employees evaluate the test results, evaluate the test itself, design and run new tests, and eventually question the big assumptions. For John, this meant signing up for other initiatives and making initial social overtures to white coworkers. At the same time, by engaging in volunteer efforts within his community outside of work, he made sure that his ties to his racial group were not compromised.

It is worth noting that revealing a big assumption doesn't necessarily mean it will be exposed as false. But even if a big assumption does contain an element of truth, an individual can often find more effective ways to operate once he or she has had a chance to challenge the assumption and its hold on his or her behavior. Indeed, John found a way to support the essence of his competing commitment—to maintain his bond with his racial group—while minimizing behavior that sabotaged his other stated commitments.

Uncovering Your Own Immunity

As you go through this process with your employees, remember that managers are every bit as susceptible to change immunity as employees are, and your competing commitments and big assumptions can have a significant impact on the people around you. Returning once more to Helen's story: When we went through this exercise with her boss, Andrew, it turned out that he was harboring some contradictions of his own. While he was committed to the success of his subordinates, Andrew at some level assumed that he alone could meet his high standards, and as a result he was laboring under a competing commitment to maintain absolute control over his projects. He was unintentionally communicating this lack of confidence to his subordinates—including Helen—in subtle ways. In the end, Andrew's and Helen's competing commitments were, without their knowledge, mutually reinforcing, keeping Helen dependent on Andrew and allowing Andrew to control her projects.

Helen and Andrew are still working through this process, but they've already gained invaluable insight into their behavior and the ways they are impeding their own progress. This may seem like a small step, but bringing these issues to the surface and confronting them head-on is challenging and painful—yet tremendously effective. It allows managers to see, at last, what's really going on when people who are genuinely committed to change nonetheless dig in their heels. It's not about identifying unproductive behavior and systematically making plans to correct it, as if treating symptoms would cure a disease. It's not about coaxing or cajoling or even giving poor performance reviews. It's about understanding the complexities of people's behavior, guiding them through a productive process to bring their competing commitments to the surface, and helping them cope with the inner conflict that is preventing them from achieving their goals.

Originally published in November 2001. Reprint R0110E

Cracking the Code
of Change

by Michael Beer and Nitin Nohria

THE NEW ECONOMY HAS ushered in great business opportunities—and great turmoil. Not since the Industrial Revolution have the stakes of dealing with change been so high. Most traditional organizations have accepted, in theory at least, that they must either change or die. And even Internet companies such as eBay, Amazon.com, and America Online recognize that they need to manage the changes associated with rapid entrepreneurial growth. Despite some individual successes, however, change remains difficult to pull off, and few companies manage the process as well as they would like. Most of their initiatives—installing new technology, downsizing, restructuring, or trying to change corporate culture—have had low success rates. The brutal fact is that about 70% of all change initiatives fail.

In our experience, the reason for most of those failures is that in their rush to change their organizations, managers end up immersing themselves in an alphabet soup of initiatives. They lose focus and become mesmerized by all the advice available in print and online about why companies should change, what they should try to accomplish, and how they should do it. This proliferation of recommendations often leads to muddle when change is attempted. The result is that most change efforts exert a heavy toll, both human and economic. To improve the odds of success, and to reduce the human carnage, it is imperative that executives understand the nature and process of corporate change much better. But even that is not enough. Leaders need to crack the code of change.

For more than 40 years now, we've been studying the nature of corporate change. And although every business's change initiative is unique, our research suggests there are two archetypes, or theories, of change. These archetypes are based on very different and often unconscious assumptions by senior executives—and the consultants and academics who advise them—about why and how changes should be made. Theory E is change based on economic value. Theory O is change based on organizational capability. Both are valid models; each theory of change achieves some of management's goals, either explicitly or implicitly. But each theory also has its costs—often unexpected ones.

Theory E change strategies are the ones that make all the headlines. In this "hard" approach to change, shareholder value is the only legitimate measure of corporate success. Change usually involves heavy use of economic incentives, drastic layoffs, downsizing, and restructuring. E change strategies are more common than O change strategies among companies in the United States, where financial markets push corporate boards for rapid turnarounds. For instance, when William A. Anders was brought in as CEO of General Dynamics in 1991, his goal was to maximize economic value—however painful the remedies might be. Over the next three years, Anders reduced the workforce by 71,000 people—44,000 through the divestiture of seven businesses and 27,000 through layoffs and attrition. Anders employed common E strategies.

Managers who subscribe to Theory O believe that if they were to focus exclusively on the price of their stock, they might harm their organizations. In this "soft" approach to change, the goal is to develop corporate culture and human capability through individual and organizational learning—the process of changing, obtaining feedback, reflecting, and making further changes. U.S. companies that adopt O strategies, as Hewlett-Packard did when its performance flagged in the 1980s, typically have strong, long-held, commitment-based psychological contracts with their employees.

Idea in Brief

Here's the brutal fact: 70% of all change initiatives fail. Why? Managers flounder in an alphabet soup of change methods, drowning in conflicting advice. Change efforts exact a heavy toll—human *and* economic—as companies flail from one change method to another.

To effect successful change, first **grasp the two basic theories of change:**

1. **Theory E** change emphasizes economic value—as measured *only* by shareholder returns. This "hard" approach boosts returns through economic incentives, drastic layoffs, and restructuring. "Chainsaw Al" Dunlop's firing 11,000 Scott Paper employees and selling several businesses—tripling shareholder value to $9 billion—is a stunning example.

2. **Theory O** change—a "softer" approach—focuses on developing corporate culture and human capability, patiently building trust and emotional commitment to the company through teamwork and communication.

Then, carefully and simultaneously **balance these very different approaches**. It's not easy. Employees distrust leaders who alternate between nurturing and cutthroat behavior. But, done well, you'll boost profits and productivity, and achieve sustainable competitive advantage.

Managers at these companies are likely to see the risks in breaking those contracts. Because they place a high value on employee commitment, Asian and European businesses are also more likely to adopt an O strategy to change.

Few companies subscribe to just one theory. Most companies we have studied have used a mix of both. But all too often, managers try to apply theories E and O in tandem without resolving the inherent tensions between them. This impulse to combine the strategies is directionally correct, but theories E and O are so different that it's hard to manage them simultaneously—employees distrust leaders who alternate between nurturing and cutthroat corporate behavior. Our research suggests, however, that there is a way to resolve the tension so that businesses can satisfy their shareholders while building viable institutions. Companies that effectively combine hard and soft approaches to change can reap big payoffs in profitability and

Idea in Practice

The UK grocery chain, ASDA, teetered on bankruptcy in 1991. Here's how CEO Archie Norman combined change Theories E and O with spectacular results: a culture of trust and openness—*and* an eightfold increase in shareholder value.

Change dimension	How to combine theories E and O	Examples from ASDA
Goals	Embrace the paradox between economic value *and* organizational capability	Norman started his tenure by stating, "Our number one objective is to secure value for our shareholders" and "We need a culture built around common ideas . . . and listening, learning, and speed of response, from the stores upwards."
Leadership	Set direction from the top *and* engage people from below	Norman unilaterally set a new pricing strategy *and* shifted power from headquarters to stores. His forthright "Tell Archie" program encouraged dialogue with all employees. He hired warm, accessible Allan Leighton to complement his own Theory O leadership style and strengthened emotional commitment to the new ASDA.
Focus	Focus on both hard and soft sides of the organization	Norman set out to win both hearts *and* minds. He boosted economic value through hard, structural changes, e.g., removing top layers of hierarchy and freezing all wages. He paid equal attention to the soft side by spending 75% of his early months as HR director creating a more egalitarian and transparent organization—"a great place for everyone to work."

Change dimension	How to combine theories E and O	Examples from ASDA
Process	Plan for spontaneity	Norman encouraged experimentation, setting up three "risk-free" stores where employees could fail without penalty. Managers experimented with store layout, product range, employee roles. A cross-functional team redesigned ASDA's entire retail organization—and produced significant innovations.
Reward system	Use incentives to reinforce rather than drive change	ASDA applied Theory E incentives in an O-like way. It encouraged all employees to participate actively in changing ASDA. And it rewarded their commitment with stock ownership and variable pay based on corporate *and* store performance.

productivity. Those companies are more likely to achieve a sustainable competitive advantage. They can also reduce the anxiety that grips whole societies in the face of corporate restructuring.

In this article, we will explore how one company successfully resolved the tensions between E and O strategies. But before we do that, we need to look at just how different the two theories are.

A Tale of Two Theories

To understand how sharply theories E and O differ, we can compare them along several key dimensions of corporate change: goals, leadership, focus, process, reward system, and use of consultants. (For a side-by-side comparison, see the table "Comparing theories of change.") We'll look at two companies in similar businesses that adopted almost pure forms of each archetype. Scott Paper successfully used Theory E to enhance shareholder value, while Champion International used Theory O to achieve a complete cultural transformation that increased its productivity and employee commitment. But as we will soon observe, both paper producers also discovered the limitations of sticking with only one theory of change. Let's compare the two companies' initiatives.

Goals

When Al Dunlap assumed leadership of Scott Paper in May 1994, he immediately fired 11,000 employees and sold off several businesses. His determination to restructure the beleaguered company was almost monomaniacal. As he said in one of his speeches: "Shareholders are the number one constituency. Show me an annual report that lists six or seven constituencies, and I'll show you a mismanaged company." From a shareholder's perspective, the results of Dunlap's actions were stunning. In just 20 months, he managed to triple shareholder returns as Scott Paper's market value rose from about $3 billion in 1994 to about $9 billion by the end of 1995. The financial community applauded his efforts and hailed Scott Paper's approach to change as a model for improving shareholder returns.

Champion's reform effort couldn't have been more different. CEO Andrew Sigler acknowledged that enhanced economic value was an appropriate target for management, but he believed that goal would be best achieved by transforming the behaviors of management, unions, and workers alike. In 1981, Sigler and other managers launched a long-term effort to restructure corporate culture around a new vision called the Champion Way, a set of values and principles designed to build up the competencies of the workforce. By improving the organization's capabilities in areas such as teamwork and communication, Sigler believed he could best increase employee productivity and thereby improve the bottom line.

Leadership

Leaders who subscribe to Theory E manage change the old-fashioned way: from the top down. They set goals with little involvement from their management teams and certainly without input from lower levels or unions. Dunlap was clearly the commander in chief at Scott Paper. The executives who survived his purges, for example, had to agree with his philosophy that shareholder value was now the company's primary objective. Nothing made clear Dunlap's leadership style better than the nickname he gloried in: "Chainsaw Al."

By contrast, participation (a Theory O trait) was the hallmark of change at Champion. Every effort was made to get all its employees emotionally committed to improving the company's performance. Teams drafted value statements, and even the industry's unions were brought into the dialogue. Employees were encouraged to identify and solve problems themselves. Change at Champion sprouted from the bottom up.

Focus

In E-type change, leaders typically focus immediately on streamlining the "hardware" of the organization—the structures and systems. These are the elements that can most easily be changed from the top down, yielding swift financial results. For instance, Dunlap quickly decided to outsource many of Scott Paper's corporate functions—benefits and payroll administration, almost all of its management information systems, some of its technology research, medical services, telemarketing, and security functions. An executive manager of a global merger explained the E rationale: "I have a [profit] goal of $176 million this year, and there's no time to involve others or develop organizational capability."

By contrast, Theory O's initial focus is on building up the "software" of an organization—the culture, behavior, and attitudes of employees. Throughout a decade of reforms, no employees were laid off at Champion. Rather, managers and employees were encouraged to collectively reexamine their work practices and behaviors with a goal of increasing productivity and quality. Managers were replaced if they did not conform to the new philosophy, but the overall firing freeze helped to create a culture of trust and commitment. Structural change followed once the culture changed. Indeed, by the mid-1990s, Champion had completely reorganized all its

Comparing theories of change

Our research has shown that all corporate transformations can be compared along the six dimensions shown here. The table outlines the differences between the E and O archetypes and illustrates what an integrated approach might look like.

Dimensions of change	Theory E	Theory O	Theories E and O combined
Goals	Maximize share-holder value	Develop organizational capabilities	Explicitly embrace the paradox between economic value and organizational capability
Leadership	Manage change from the top down	Encourage participation from the bottom up	Set direction from the top and engage the people below
Focus	Emphasize structure and systems	Build up corporate culture: employees' behavior and attitudes	Focus simultaneously on the hard (structures and systems) and the soft (corporate culture)
Process	Plan and establish programs	Experiment and evolve	Plan for spontaneity
Reward system	Motivate through financial incentives	Motivate through commitment—use pay as fair exchange	Use incentives to reinforce change but not to drive it
Use of consultants	Consultants analyze problems and shape solutions	Consultants support management in shaping their own solutions	Consultants are expert resources who empower employees

corporate functions. Once a hierarchical, functionally organized company, Champion adopted a matrix structure that empowered employee teams to focus more on customers.

Process

Theory E is predicated on the view that no battle can be won without a clear, comprehensive, common plan of action that encourages internal coordination and inspires confidence among customers, suppliers, and investors. The plan lets leaders quickly motivate and mobilize their businesses; it compels them to take tough, decisive actions they presumably haven't taken in the past. The changes at Scott Paper unfolded like a military battle plan. Managers were instructed to achieve specific targets by specific dates. If they didn't adhere to Dunlap's tightly choreographed marching orders, they risked being fired.

Meanwhile, the changes at Champion were more evolutionary and emergent than planned and programmatic. When the company's decade-long reform began in 1981, there was no master blueprint. The idea was that innovative work processes, values, and culture changes in one plant would be adapted and used by other plants on their way through the corporate system. No single person, not even Sigler, was seen as the driver of change. Instead, local leaders took responsibility. Top management simply encouraged experimentation from the ground up, spread new ideas to other workers, and transferred managers of innovative units to lagging ones.

Reward System
The rewards for managers in E-type change programs are primarily financial. Employee compensation, for example, is linked with financial incentives, mainly stock options. Dunlap's own compensation package—which ultimately netted him more than $100 million—was tightly linked to shareholders' interests. Proponents of this system argue that financial incentives guarantee that employees' interests match stockholders' interests. Financial rewards also help top executives feel compensated for a difficult job—one in which they are often reviled by their onetime colleagues and the larger community.

The O-style compensation systems at Champion reinforced the goals of culture change, but they didn't drive those goals. A skills-based pay system and a corporatewide gains-sharing plan were installed to draw union workers and management into a community of purpose. Financial incentives were used only as a supplement to those systems and not to push particular reforms. While Champion did offer a companywide bonus to achieve business goals in two separate years, this came late in the change process and played a minor role in actually fulfilling those goals.

Use of Consultants

Theory E change strategies often rely heavily on external consultants. A SWAT team of Ivy League–educated MBAs, armed with an arsenal of state-of-the-art ideas, is brought in to find new ways to look at the business and manage it. The consultants can help CEOs get a fix on urgent issues and priorities. They also offer much-needed political and psychological support for CEOs who are under fire from financial markets. At Scott Paper, Dunlap engaged consultants to identify many of the painful cost-savings initiatives that he subsequently implemented.

Theory O change programs rely far less on consultants. The handful of consultants who were introduced at Champion helped managers and workers make their own business analyses and craft their own solutions. And while the consultants had their own ideas, they did not recommend any corporate program, dictate any solutions, or whip anyone into line. They simply led a process of discovery and learning that was intended to change the corporate culture in a way that could not be foreseen at the outset.

In their purest forms, both change theories clearly have their limitations. CEOs who must make difficult E-style choices understandably distance themselves from their employees to ease their own pain and guilt. Once removed from their people, these CEOs begin to see their employees as part of the problem. As time goes on, these leaders become less and less inclined to adopt O-style change strategies. They fail to invest in building the company's human resources, which inevitably hollows out the company and saps its capacity for sustained performance. At Scott Paper, for example, Dunlap trebled shareholder returns but failed to build the capabilities needed for sustained competitive advantage—commitment, coordination, communication, and creativity. In 1995, Dunlap sold Scott Paper to its longtime competitor Kimberly-Clark.

CEOs who embrace Theory O find that their loyalty and commitment to their employees can prevent them from making tough decisions. The temptation is to postpone the bitter medicine in the hopes that rising productivity will improve the business situation. But productivity gains aren't enough when fundamental structural change is required. That reality is underscored by today's global financial system, which makes corporate performance instantly transparent to large institutional shareholders whose fund managers are under enormous pressure to show good results. Consider Champion. By 1997, it had become one of the leaders in its industry based on most performance measures. Still, newly instated CEO Richard Olsen was forced to admit a tough reality: Champion shareholders had not seen a significant increase in the economic value of the company in more than a decade. Indeed, when Champion was sold recently to Finland-based UPM-Kymmene, it was acquired for a mere 1.5 times its original share value.

Managing the Contradictions

Clearly, if the objective is to build a company that can adapt, survive, and prosper over the years, Theory E strategies must somehow be combined with Theory O strategies. But unless they're carefully handled, melding E and O is likely to bring the worst of both theories and the benefits of neither. Indeed, the corporate changes we've studied that arbitrarily and haphazardly mixed E and O techniques proved destabilizing to the organizations in which they were imposed. Managers in those companies would certainly have been better off to pick either pure E or pure O strategies—with all their costs. At least one set of stakeholders would have benefited.

The obvious way to combine E and O is to sequence them. Some companies, notably General Electric, have done this quite successfully. At GE, CEO Jack Welch began his sequenced change by imposing an E-type restructuring. He demanded that all GE businesses be first or second in their industries. Any unit that failed that test would be fixed, sold off, or closed. Welch followed that up with a massive downsizing of the GE bureaucracy. Between 1981 and 1985, total employment at the corporation dropped from 412,000 to 299,000. Sixty percent of the corporate staff, mostly in planning and finance, was laid off. In this phase, GE people began to call Welch "Neutron Jack," after the fabled bomb that was designed to destroy people but leave buildings intact. Once he had wrung out the redundancies, however, Welch adopted an O strategy. In 1985, he started a series of organizational initiatives to change GE culture. He declared that the company had to become "boundaryless," and unit leaders across the corporation had to submit to being challenged by their subordinates in open forum. Feedback and open communication eventually eroded the hierarchy. Soon Welch applied the new order to GE's global businesses.

Unfortunately for companies like Champion, sequenced change is far easier if you begin, as Welch did, with Theory E. Indeed, it is highly unlikely that E would successfully follow O because of the sense of betrayal that would involve. It is hard to imagine how a draconian program of layoffs and downsizing can leave intact the psychological contract and culture a company has so patiently built up over the years. But whatever the order, one sure problem with sequencing is that it can take a very long time; at GE it has taken almost two decades. A sequenced change may also require two CEOs, carefully chosen for their contrasting styles and philosophies, which may create its own set of problems. Most turnaround managers don't survive restructuring—partly because of their own inflexibility and partly because they can't live down the distrust that their ruthlessness has earned them. In most cases, even the best-intentioned effort to rebuild trust and commitment rarely overcomes a bloody past. Welch is the exception that proves the rule.

So what should you do? How can you achieve rapid improvements in economic value while simultaneously developing an open, trusting corporate culture? Paradoxical as those goals may appear, our research shows that it is possible to apply theories E and O together. It requires great will, skill—and wisdom. But precisely because it is more difficult than mere sequencing, the simultaneous use of O and E strategies is more likely to be a source of sustainable competitive advantage.

One company that exemplifies the reconciliation of the hard and soft approaches is ASDA, the UK grocery chain that CEO Archie

Norman took over in December 1991, when the retailer was nearly bankrupt. Norman laid off employees, flattened the organization, and sold off losing businesses—acts that usually spawn distrust among employees and distance executives from their people. Yet during Norman's eight-year tenure as CEO, ASDA also became famous for its atmosphere of trust and openness. It has been described by executives at Wal-Mart—itself famous for its corporate culture—as being "more like Wal-Mart than we are." Let's look at how ASDA resolved the conflicts of E and O along the six main dimensions of change.

Explicitly confront the tension between E and O goals

With his opening speech to ASDA's executive team—none of whom he had met—Norman indicated clearly that he intended to apply both E and O strategies in his change effort. It is doubtful that any of his listeners fully understood him at the time, but it was important that he had no conflicts about recognizing the paradox between the two strategies for change. He said as much in his maiden speech: "Our number one objective is to secure value for our shareholders and secure the trading future of the business. I am not coming in with any magical solutions. I intend to spend the next few weeks listening and forming ideas for our precise direction. . . . We need a culture built around common ideas and goals that include listening, learning, and speed of response, from the stores upwards. [But] there will be management reorganization. My objective is to establish a clear focus on the stores, shorten lines of communication, and build one team." If there is a contradiction between building a high-involvement organization and restructuring to enhance shareholder value, Norman embraced it.

Set direction from the top and engage people below

From day one, Norman set strategy without expecting any participation from below. He said ASDA would adopt an everyday-low-pricing strategy, and Norman unilaterally determined that change would begin by having two experimental store formats up and running within six months. He decided to shift power from the headquarters to the stores, declaring: "I want everyone to be close to the stores.

We must love the stores to death; that is our business." But even from the start, there was an O quality to Norman's leadership style. As he put it in his first speech: "First, I am forthright, and I like to argue. Second, I want to discuss issues as colleagues. I am looking for your advice and your disagreement." Norman encouraged dialogue with employees and customers through colleague and customer circles. He set up a "Tell Archie" program so that people could voice their concerns and ideas.

Making way for opposite leadership styles was also an essential ingredient to Norman's—and ASDA's—success. This was most clear in Norman's willingness to hire Allan Leighton shortly after he took over. Leighton eventually became deputy chief executive. Norman and Leighton shared the same E and O values, but they had completely different personalities and styles. Norman, cool and reserved, impressed people with the power of his mind—his intelligence and business acumen. Leighton, who is warmer and more people oriented, worked on employees' emotions with the power of his personality. As one employee told us, "People respect Archie, but they love Allan." Norman was the first to credit Leighton with having helped to create emotional commitment to the new ASDA. While it might be possible for a single individual to embrace opposite leadership styles, accepting an equal partner with a very different personality makes it easier to capitalize on those styles. Leighton certainly helped Norman reach out to the organization. Together they held quarterly meetings with store managers to hear their ideas, and they supplemented those meetings with impromptu talks.

Focus simultaneously on the hard and soft sides of the organization

Norman's immediate actions followed both the E goal of increasing economic value and the O goal of transforming culture. On the E side, Norman focused on structure. He removed layers of hierarchy at the top of the organization, fired the financial officer who had been part of ASDA's disastrous policies, and decreed a wage freeze for everyone—management and workers alike. But from the start, the O strategy was an equal part of Norman's plan. He bought time for all this change by warning the markets that financial recovery would take three years. Norman later said that he spent 75% of his early months at ASDA as the company's human resource director, making the organization less hierarchical, more egalitarian, and more transparent. Both Norman and Leighton were keenly aware that they had to win hearts and minds. As Norman put it to workers: "We need to make ASDA a great place for everyone to work."

Plan for spontaneity

Training programs, total-quality programs, and top-driven culture change programs played little part in ASDA's transformation. From the start, the ASDA change effort was set up to encourage experimentation and evolution. To promote learning, for example, ASDA set up an experimental store that was later expanded to three stores. It was declared a risk-free zone, meaning there would be no penalties for failure. A cross-functional task force "renewed," or redesigned, ASDA's entire retail proposition, its organization, and its managerial structure. Store managers were encouraged to experiment with store layout, employee roles, ranges of products offered, and so on. The experiments produced significant innovations in all aspects of store operations. ASDA's managers learned, for example, that they couldn't renew a store unless that store's management team was ready for new ideas. This led to an innovation called the Driving Test, which assessed whether store managers' skills in leading the change process were aligned with the intended changes. The test perfectly illustrates how E and O can come together: it bubbled up O-style from the bottom of the company, yet it bound managers in an E-type contract. Managers who failed the test were replaced.

Let incentives reinforce change, not drive it

Any synthesis of E and O must recognize that compensation is a double-edged sword. Money can focus and motivate managers, but it can also hamper teamwork, commitment, and learning. The way to resolve this dilemma is to apply Theory E incentives in an O way. Employees' high involvement is encouraged to develop their commitment to change, and variable pay is used to reward that commitment.

ASDA's senior executives were compensated with stock options that were tied to the company's value. These helped attract key executives to ASDA. Unlike most E-strategy companies, however, ASDA had a stock-ownership plan for all employees. In addition, store-level employees got variable pay based on both corporate performance and their stores' records. In the end, compensation represented a fair exchange of value between the company and its individual employees. But Norman believed that compensation had not played a major role in motivating change at the company.

Use consultants as expert resources who empower employees
Consultants can provide specialized knowledge and technical skills that the company doesn't have, particularly in the early stages of organizational change. Management's task is figuring out how to use those resources without abdicating leadership of the change effort. ASDA followed the middle ground between Theory E and Theory O. It made limited use of four consulting firms in the early stages of its transformation. The consulting firms always worked alongside management and supported its leadership of change. However, their engagement was intentionally cut short by Norman to prevent ASDA and its managers from becoming dependent on the consultants. For example, an expert in store organization was hired to support the task force assigned to renew ASDA's first few experimental stores, but later stores were renewed without his involvement.

By embracing the paradox inherent in simultaneously employing E and O change theories, Norman and Leighton transformed ASDA to the advantage of its shareholders and employees. The organization went through personnel changes, unit sell-offs, and hierarchical upheaval. Yet these potentially destructive actions did not prevent ASDA's employees from committing to change and the new corporate culture because Norman and Leighton had won employees' trust by constantly listening, debating, and being willing to learn. Candid about their intentions from the outset, they balanced the tension between the two change theories.

By 1999, the company had multiplied shareholder value eight-fold. The organizational capabilities built by Norman and Leighton

Change Theories in the New Economy

HISTORICALLY, THE STUDY of change has been restricted to mature, large companies that needed to reverse their competitive declines. But the arguments we have advanced in this article also apply to entrepreneurial companies that need to manage rapid growth. Here, too, we believe that the most successful strategy for change will be one that combines theories E and O.

Just as there are two ways of changing, so there are two kinds of entrepreneurs. One group subscribes to an ideology akin to Theory E. Their primary goal is to prepare for a cash-out, such as an IPO or an acquisition by an established player. Maximizing market value before the cash-out is their sole and abiding purpose. These entrepreneurs emphasize shaping the firm's strategy, structure, and systems to build a quick, strong market presence. Mercurial leaders who drive the company using a strong top-down style are typically at the helm of such companies. They lure others to join them using high-powered incentives such as stock options. The goal is to get rich quick.

Other entrepreneurs, however, are driven by an ideology more akin to Theory O—the building of an institution. Accumulating wealth is important, but it is secondary to creating a company that is based on a deeply held set of values and that has a strong culture. These entrepreneurs are likely to subscribe to an egalitarian style that invites everyone's participation. They look to attract others who share their passion about the cause—though they certainly provide generous stock options as well. The goal in this case is to make a difference, not just to make money.

Many people fault entrepreneurs who are driven by a Theory E view of the world. But we can think of other entrepreneurs who have destroyed businesses because they were overly wrapped up in the Theory O pursuit of a higher ideal and didn't pay attention to the pragmatics of the market. Steve Jobs's venture, Next, comes to mind. Both types of entrepreneurs have to find some way of tapping the qualities of theories E and O, just as large companies do.

---

also gave ASDA the sustainable competitive advantage that Dunlap had been unable to build at Scott Paper and that Sigler had been unable to build at Champion. While Dunlap was forced to sell a demoralized and ineffective organization to Kimberly-Clark, and while a languishing Champion was sold to UPM-Kymmene, Norman and Leighton in June 1999 found a friendly and culturally compatible suitor in Wal-Mart, which was willing to pay a substantial premium for the organizational capabilities that ASDA had so painstakingly developed.

In the end, the integration of theories E and O created major change—and major payoffs—for ASDA. Such payoffs are possible for other organizations that want to develop a sustained advantage in today's economy. But that advantage can come only from a constant willingness and ability to develop organizations for the long term combined with a constant monitoring of shareholder value—E dancing with O, in an unending minuet.

Originally published in May 2000. Reprint R00301

The Hard Side of Change Management

by Harold L. Sirkin, Perry Keenan, and Alan Jackson

WHEN FRENCH NOVELIST JEAN-BAPTISTE Alphonse Karr wrote *"Plus ça change, plus c'est la même chose,"* he could have been penning an epigram about change management. For over three decades, academics, managers, and consultants, realizing that transforming organizations is difficult, have dissected the subject. They've sung the praises of leaders who communicate vision and walk the talk in order to make change efforts succeed. They've sanctified the importance of changing organizational culture and employees' attitudes. They've teased out the tensions between top-down transformation efforts and participatory approaches to change. And they've exhorted companies to launch campaigns that appeal to people's hearts and minds. Still, studies show that in most organizations, two out of three transformation initiatives fail. The more things change, the more they stay the same.

Managing change *is* tough, but part of the problem is that there is little agreement on what factors most influence transformation initiatives. Ask five executives to name the one factor critical for the success of these programs, and you'll probably get five different answers. That's because each manager looks at an initiative from his or her viewpoint and, based on personal experience, focuses on different success factors. The experts, too, offer different perspectives. A recent search on Amazon.com for books on "change and management" turned up 6,153 titles, each with a distinct take on the topic. Those ideas have a lot to offer, but taken together, they force companies to tackle many priorities simultaneously, which spreads resources and skills thin. Moreover, executives use different approaches in different parts of the organization, which compounds the turmoil that usually accompanies change.

In recent years, many change management gurus have focused on soft issues, such as culture, leadership, and motivation. Such elements are important for success, but managing these aspects alone isn't sufficient to implement transformation projects. Soft factors don't directly influence the outcomes of many change programs. For instance, visionary leadership is often vital for transformation projects, but not always. The same can be said about communication with employees. Moreover, it isn't easy to change attitudes or relationships; they're deeply ingrained in organizations and people. And although changes in, say, culture or motivation levels can be indirectly gauged through surveys and interviews, it's tough to get reliable data on soft factors.

What's missing, we believe, is a focus on the not-so-fashionable aspects of change management: the hard factors. These factors bear three distinct characteristics. First, companies are able to measure them in direct or indirect ways. Second, companies can easily communicate their importance, both within and outside organizations. Third, and perhaps most important, businesses are capable of influencing those elements quickly. Some of the hard factors that affect a transformation initiative are the time necessary to complete it, the number of people required to execute it, and the financial results that intended actions are expected to achieve. Our research shows that change projects fail to get off the ground when companies neglect the hard factors. That doesn't mean that executives can ignore the soft elements; that would be a grave mistake. However, if companies don't pay attention to the hard issues first, transformation programs will break down before the soft elements come into play.

Idea in Brief

Two out of every three transformation programs fail. Why? Companies overemphasize the soft side of change: leadership style, corporate culture, employee motivation. Though these elements are critical for success, change projects can't get off the ground unless companies address harder elements first.

The essential hard elements? Think of them as DICE:

- **Duration:** time between milestone reviews—the shorter, the better

- **Integrity:** project teams' skill

- **Commitment:** senior executives' and line managers' dedication to the program

- **Effort:** the extra work employees must do to adopt new processes—the less, the better

By assessing each DICE element *before* you launch a major change initiative, you can identify potential problem areas and make the necessary adjustments (such as reconfiguring a project team's composition or reallocating resources) to ensure the program's success. You can also use DICE *after* launching a project—to make midcourse corrections if the initiative veers off track.

DICE helps companies lay the foundation for successful change. Using the DICE assessment technique, one global beverage company executed a multiproject organization-wide change program that generated hundreds of millions of dollars, breathed new life into its once-stagnant brands, and cracked open new markets.

That's a lesson we learned when we identified the common denominators of change. In 1992, we started with the contrarian hypothesis that organizations handle transformations in remarkably similar ways. We researched projects in a number of industries and countries to identify those common elements. Our initial 225-company study revealed a consistent correlation between the outcomes (success or failure) of change programs and four hard factors: project *duration,* particularly the time between project reviews; performance *integrity,* or the capabilities of project teams; the *commitment* of both senior executives and the staff whom the change will affect the most; and the additional *effort* that employees must make to cope with the change. We called these variables the DICE factors because we could load them in favor of projects' success.

Idea in Practice

Conducting a DICE Assessment

Your project has the greatest chance of success if the following hard elements are in place:

Duration

A long project reviewed frequently stands a far better chance of succeeding than a short project reviewed infrequently. Problems can be identified at the first sign of trouble, allowing for prompt corrective actions. Review complex projects every two weeks; more straightforward initiatives, every six to eight weeks.

Integrity

A change program's success hinges on a high-integrity, high-quality project team. To identify team candidates with the right portfolio of skills, solicit names from key colleagues, including top performers in functions other than your own. Recruit people who have problem-solving skills, are results oriented, and are methodical but tolerate ambiguity. Look also for organizational savvy, willingness to accept responsibility for decisions, and a disdain for the limelight.

Commitment

If employees don't see company leaders supporting a change initiative, they won't change. Visibly endorse the initiative—no amount of public support is too much. When you feel you're "talking up" a change effort at least three times more than you need to, you've hit it right.

Also continually communicate why the change is needed and what it

We completed our study in 1994, and in the 11 years since then, the Boston Consulting Group has used those four factors to predict the outcomes, and guide the execution, of more than 1,000 change management initiatives worldwide. Not only has the correlation held, but no other factors (or combination of factors) have predicted outcomes as well.

The Four Key Factors

If you think about it, the different ways in which organizations combine the four factors create a continuum—from projects that are set up to succeed to those that are set up to fail. At one extreme, a short means for employees. Ensure that all messages about the change are consistent and clear. Reach out to managers and employees through one-on-one conversations to win them over.

Effort

If adopting a change burdens employees with too much additional effort, they'll resist. Calculate how much work employees will have to do beyond their existing responsibilities to implement the change. Ensure that no one's workload increases more than 10%. If necessary, remove nonessential regular work from employees with key roles in the transformation project. Use temporary workers or outsource some processes to accommodate additional workload.

Using the DICE Framework

Conducting a DICE assessment fosters successful change by sparking valuable senior leadership debate about project strategy It also improves change effectiveness by enabling companies to manage large portfolios of projects.

Example: A manufacturing company planned 40 projects as part of a profitability-improvement program. After conducting a DICE assessment for each project, leaders and project owners identified the five most important projects and asked, "How can we ensure these projects' success?" They moved people around on teams, reconfigured some projects, and identified initiatives senior managers should pay more attention to—setting up their most crucial projects for resounding success.

project led by a skilled, motivated, and cohesive team, championed by top management and implemented in a department that is receptive to the change and has to put in very little additional effort, is bound to succeed. At the other extreme, a long, drawn-out project executed by an inexpert, unenthusiastic, and disjointed team, without any top-level sponsors and targeted at a function that dislikes the change and has to do a lot of extra work, will fail. Businesses can easily identify change programs at either end of the spectrum, but most initiatives occupy the middle ground where the likelihood of success or failure is difficult to assess. Executives must study the four DICE factors carefully to figure out if their change programs will fly—or die.

The Four Factors

THESE FACTORS determine the outcome of any transformation initiative.

D. The **duration** of time until the change program is completed if it has a short life span; if not short, the amount of time between reviews of milestones.

I. The project team's performance **integrity**; that is, its ability to complete the initiative on time. That depends on members' skills and traits relative to the project's requirements.

C. The **commitment** to change that top management (C1) and employees affected by the change (C2) display.

E. The **effort** over and above the usual work that the change initiative demands of employees.

Duration

Companies make the mistake of worrying mostly about the time it will take to implement change programs. They assume that the longer an initiative carries on, the more likely it is to fail—the early impetus will peter out, windows of opportunity will close, objectives will be forgotten, key supporters will leave or lose their enthusiasm, and problems will accumulate. However, contrary to popular perception, our studies show that a long project that is reviewed frequently is more likely to succeed than a short project that isn't reviewed frequently. Thus, the time between reviews is more critical for success than a project's life span.

Companies should formally review transformation projects at least bimonthly since, in our experience, the probability that change initiatives will run into trouble rises exponentially when the time between reviews exceeds eight weeks. Whether reviews should be scheduled even more frequently depends on how long executives feel the project can carry on without going off track. Complex projects should be reviewed fortnightly; more familiar or straightforward initiatives can be assessed every six to eight weeks.

Scheduling milestones and assessing their impact are the best way by which executives can review the execution of projects, identify gaps, and spot new risks. The most effective milestones are those that describe major actions or achievements rather than day-to-day activities. They must enable senior executives and project sponsors to confirm that the project has made progress since the last review took place. Good milestones encompass a number of tasks that teams must complete. For example, describing a particular milestone as "Consultations with Stakeholders Completed" is more effective than "Consult Stakeholders" because it represents an achievement and shows that the project has made headway. Moreover, it suggests that several activities were completed—identifying stakeholders, assessing their needs, and talking to them about the project. When a milestone looks as though it won't be reached on time, the project team must try to understand why, take corrective actions, and learn from the experience to prevent problems from recurring.

Review of such a milestone—what we refer to as a "learning milestone"—isn't an impromptu assessment of the Monday-morning kind. It should be a formal occasion during which senior-management sponsors and the project team evaluate the latter's performance on all the dimensions that have a bearing on success and failure. The team must provide a concise report of its progress, and members and sponsors must check if the team is on track to complete, or has finished all the tasks to deliver, the milestone. They should also determine whether achieving the milestone has had the desired effect on the company; discuss the problems the team faced in reaching the milestone; and determine how that accomplishment will affect the next phase of the project. Sponsors and team members must have the power to address weaknesses. When necessary, they should alter processes, agree to push for more or different resources, or suggest a new direction. At these meetings, senior executives must pay special attention to the dynamics within teams, changes in the organization's perceptions about the initiative, and communications from the top.

Integrity

By performance integrity, we mean the extent to which companies can rely on teams of managers, supervisors, and staff to execute change projects successfully. In a perfect world, every team would be flawless, but no business has enough great people to ensure that. Besides, senior executives are often reluctant to allow star performers to join change efforts because regular work can suffer. But since the success of change programs depends on the quality of teams, companies must free up the best staff while making sure that day-to-day operations don't falter. In companies that have succeeded in implementing change programs, we find that employees go the extra mile to ensure their day-to-day work gets done.

Since project teams handle a wide range of activities, resources, pressures, external stimuli, and unforeseen obstacles, they must be cohesive and well led. It's not enough for senior executives to ask people at the watercooler if a project team is doing well; they must clarify members' roles, commitments, and accountability. They must choose the team leader and, most important, work out the team's composition.

Smart executive sponsors, we find, are very inclusive when picking teams. They identify talent by soliciting names from key colleagues, including human resource managers; by circulating criteria they have drawn up; and by looking for top performers in all functions. While they accept volunteers, they take care not to choose only supporters of the change initiative. Senior executives personally interview people so that they can construct the right portfolio of skills, knowledge, and social networks. They also decide if potential team members should commit all their time to the project; if not, they must ask them to allocate specific days or times of the day to the initiative. Top management makes public the parameters on which it will judge the team's performance and how that evaluation fits into the company's regular appraisal process. Once the project gets under way, sponsors must measure the cohesion of teams by administering confidential surveys to solicit members' opinions.

Executives often make the mistake of assuming that because someone is a good, well-liked manager, he or she will also make a decent team leader. That sounds reasonable, but effective managers of the status quo aren't necessarily good at changing organizations. Usually, good team leaders have problem-solving skills, are results oriented, are methodical in their approach but tolerate ambiguity, are organizationally savvy, are willing to accept responsibility for decisions, and while being highly motivated, don't crave the limelight. A CEO who successfully led two major transformation projects in the past ten years used these six criteria to quiz senior executives about the caliber of nominees for project teams. The top management team rejected one in three candidates, on average, before finalizing the teams.

Commitment

Companies must boost the commitment of two different groups of people if they want change projects to take root: They must get visible backing from the most influential executives (what we call C1), who are not necessarily those with the top titles. And they must take into account the enthusiasm—or often, lack thereof—of the people who must deal with the new systems, processes, or ways of working (C2).

Top-level commitment is vital to engendering commitment from those at the coal face. If employees don't see that the company's leadership is backing a project, they're unlikely to change. No amount of top-level support is too much. In 1999, when we were working with the CEO of a consumer products company, he told us that he was doing much more than necessary to display his support for a nettlesome project. When we talked to line managers, they said that the CEO had extended very little backing for the project. They felt that if he wanted the project to succeed, he would have to support it more visibly! A rule of thumb: When you feel that you are talking up a change initiative at least three times more than you need to, your managers will feel that you are backing the transformation.

Sometimes, senior executives are reluctant to back initiatives. That's understandable; they're often bringing about changes that may negatively affect employees' jobs and lives. However, if senior executives do not communicate the need for change, and what it means for employees, they endanger their projects' success. In one financial services firm, top management's commitment to a program that would improve cycle times, reduce errors, and slash costs was low because it entailed layoffs. Senior executives found it gut-wrenching to talk about layoffs in an organization that had prided itself on being a place where good people could find lifetime employment. However, the CEO realized that he needed to tackle the thorny issues around the layoffs to get the project implemented on schedule. He tapped a senior company veteran to organize a series of speeches and meetings in order to provide consistent explanations for the layoffs, the timing, the consequences for job security, and so on. He also appointed a well-respected general manager to lead the change program. Those actions reassured employees that the organization would tackle the layoffs in a professional and humane fashion.

Companies often underestimate the role that managers and staff play in transformation efforts. By communicating with them too late or inconsistently, senior executives end up alienating the people who are most affected by the changes. It's surprising how often something senior executives believe is a good thing is seen by staff as a bad thing, or a message that senior executives think is perfectly clear is misunderstood. That usually happens when senior executives articulate subtly different versions of critical messages. For instance, in one company that applied the DICE framework, scores for a project showed a low degree of staff commitment. It turned out that these employees had become confused, even distrustful, because one senior manager had said, "Layoffs will not occur," while another had said, "They are not expected to occur."

Organizations also underestimate their ability to build staff support. A simple effort to reach out to employees can turn them into champions of new ideas. For example, in the 1990s, a major American energy producer was unable to get the support of mid-level managers, supervisors, and workers for a productivity improvement program. After trying several times, the company's senior executives decided to hold a series of one-on-one conversations with mid-level managers in a last-ditch effort to win them over. The conversations focused on the program's objectives, its impact on employees, and why the organization might not be able to survive without the changes. Partly because of the straight talk, the initiative gained some momentum. This allowed a project team to demonstrate a series of quick wins, which gave the initiative a new lease on life.

Effort

When companies launch transformation efforts, they frequently don't realize, or know how to deal with the fact, that employees are already busy with their day-to-day responsibilities. According to staffing tables, people in many businesses work 80-plus-hour weeks. If, on top of existing responsibilities, line managers and staff have to deal with changes to their work or to the systems they use, they will resist.

Project teams must calculate how much work employees will have to do beyond their existing responsibilities to change over to new processes. Ideally, no one's workload should increase more than 10%. Go beyond that, and the initiative will probably run into trouble. Resources will become overstretched and compromise either the change program or normal operations. Employee morale will fall, and conflict may arise between teams and line staff. To minimize the dangers, project managers should use a simple metric like the percentage increase in effort the employees who must cope with the new ways feel they must contribute. They should also check if the additional effort they have demanded comes on top of heavy workloads and if employees are likely to resist the project because it will demand more of their scarce time.

Companies must decide whether to take away some of the regular work of employees who will play key roles in the transformation project. Companies can start by ridding these employees of discretionary or nonessential responsibilities. In addition, firms should review all the other projects in the operating plan and assess which ones are critical for the change effort. At one company, the project steering committee delayed or restructured 120 out of 250 subprojects so that some line managers could focus on top-priority projects. Another way to relieve pressure is for the company to bring in temporary workers, like retired managers, to carry out routine activities or to outsource current processes until the changeover is complete. Handing off routine work or delaying projects is costly and time-consuming, so companies need to think through such issues before kicking off transformation efforts.

Calculating DICE Scores

COMPANIES CAN DETERMINE if their change programs will succeed by asking executives to calculate scores for each of the four factors of the DICE framework—duration, integrity, commitment, and effort. They must grade each factor on a scale from 1 to 4 (using fractions, if necessary); the lower the score, the better. Thus, a score of 1 suggests that the factor is highly likely to contribute to the program's success, and a score of 4 means that it is highly unlikely to contribute to success. We find that the following questions and scoring guidelines allow executives to rate transformation initiatives effectively:

Duration [D]

Ask: Do formal project reviews occur regularly? If the project will take more than two months to complete, what is the average time between reviews?

Score: If the time between project reviews is less than two months, you should give the project 1 point. If the time is between two and four months, you should award the project 2 points; between four and eight months, 3 points; and if reviews are more than eight months apart, give the project 4 points.

Integrity of Performance [i]

Ask: Is the team leader capable? How strong are team members' skills and motivations? Do they have sufficient time to spend on the change initiative?

Score: If the project team is led by a highly capable leader who is respected by peers, if the members have the skills and motivation to complete the project in the stipulated time frame, and if the company has assigned at least 50% of the team members' time to the project, you can give the project 1 point. If the team is lacking on all those dimensions, you should award the project 4 points. If the team's capabilities are somewhere in between, assign the project 2 or 3 points.

Senior Management Commitment [C_1]

Ask: Do senior executives regularly communicate the reason for the change and the importance of its success? Is the message convincing? Is the message consistent, both across the top management team and over time? Has top management devoted enough resources to the change program?

Score: If senior management has, through actions and words, clearly communicated the need for change, you must give the project 1 point. If senior executives appear to be neutral, it gets 2 or 3 points. If managers perceive senior executives to be reluctant to support the change, award the project 4 points.

Local-Level Commitment [C_2]

Ask: Do the employees most affected by the change understand the reason for it and believe it's worthwhile? Are they enthusiastic and supportive or worried and obstructive?

Score: If employees are eager to take on the change initiative, you can give the project 1 point, and if they are just willing, 2 points. If they're reluctant or strongly reluctant, you should award the project 3 or 4 points.

Effort [E]

Ask: What is the percentage of increased effort that employees must make to implement the change effort? Does the incremental effort come on top of a heavy workload? Have people strongly resisted the increased demands on them?

Score: If the project requires less than 10% extra work by employees, you can give it 1 point. If it's 10% to 20% extra, it should get 2 points. If it's 20% to 40%, it must be 3 points. And if it's more than 40% additional work, you should give the project 4 points.

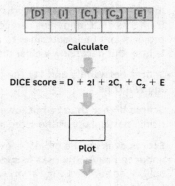

[D]	[I]	[C_1]	[C_2]	[E]

Calculate

$$\text{DICE score} = D + 2I + 2C_1 + C_2 + E$$

Plot

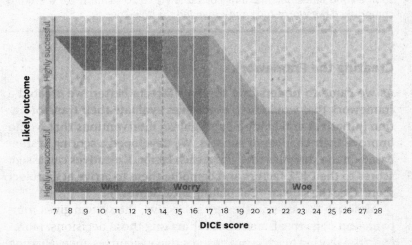

DICE score

Calculating DICE Scores (continued)

Executives can combine the four elements into a project score. When we conducted a regression analysis of our database of change efforts, we found that the combination that correlates most closely with actual outcomes doubles the weight given to team performance (I) and senior management commitment (C1). That translates into the following formula:

DICE Score = D + (2 x I) + (2 x C_1) + C_2 + E

In the 1-to-4 scoring system, the formula generates overall scores that range from 7 to 28. Companies can compare a project's score with those of past projects and their outcomes to assess if the project is slated for success or failure. Our data show a clear distribution of scores:

Scores between 7 and 14: The project is very likely to succeed. We call this the Win Zone.

Scores higher than 14 but lower than 17: Risks to the project's success are rising, particularly as the score approaches 17. This is the Worry Zone.

Scores over 17: The project is extremely risky. If a project scores over 17 and under 19 points, the risks to success are very high. Beyond 19, the project is unlikely to succeed. That's why we call this the Woe Zone.

We have changed the boundaries of the zones over time. For instance, the Worry Zone was between 14 and 21 points at first, and the Woe Zone from 21 to 28 points. But we found that companies prefer to be alerted to trouble as soon as outcomes become unpredictable (17 to 20 points). We therefore compressed the Worry Zone and expanded the Woe Zone.

Creating the Framework

As we came to understand the four factors better, we created a framework that would help executives evaluate their transformation initiatives and shine a spotlight on interventions that would improve their chances of success. We developed a scoring system based on the variables that affect each factor. Executives can assign scores to the DICE factors and combine them to arrive at a project score. (See the sidebar "Calculating DICE Scores.")

Although the assessments are subjective, the system gives companies an objective framework for making those decisions. Moreover, the scoring mechanism ensures that executives are evaluating projects and making trade-offs more consistently across projects.

A company can compare its DICE score on the day it kicks off a project with the scores of previous projects, as well as their outcomes, to check if the initiative has been set up for success. When we calculated the scores of the 225 change projects in our database and compared them with the outcomes, the analysis was compelling. Projects clearly fell into three categories, or zones: *Win,* which means that any project with a score in that range is statistically likely to succeed; *worry,* which suggests that the project's outcome is hard to predict; and *woe,* which implies that the project is totally unpredictable or fated for mediocrity or failure. (See the figure "DICE scores predict project outcomes.")

Companies can track how change projects are faring by calculating scores over time or before and after they have made changes to a

DICE scores predict project outcomes

When we plotted the DICE scores of 225 change management initiatives on the horizontal axis, and the outcomes of those projects on the vertical axis, we found three sets of correlations. Projects with DICE scores between 7 and 14 were usually successful; those with scores over 14 and under 17 were unpredictable; and projects with scores over 17 were usually unsuccessful. We named the three zones Win, Worry, and Woe, respectively. (Each number plotted on the graph represents the number of projects, out of the 225 projects, having a particular DICE score.)

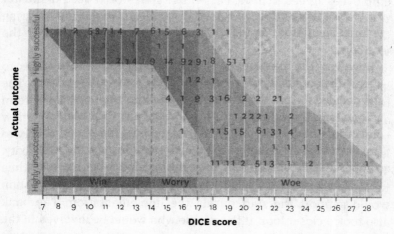

project's structure. The four factors offer a litmus test that executives can use to assess the probability of success for a given project or set of projects. Consider the case of a large Australian bank that in 1994 wanted to restructure its back-office operations. Senior executives agreed on the rationale for the change but differed on whether the bank could achieve its objectives, since the transformation required major changes in processes and organizational structures. Bringing the team and the senior executives together long enough to sort out their differences proved impossible; people were just too busy. That's when the project team decided to analyze the initiative using the DICE framework.

Doing so condensed what could have been a free-flowing two-day debate into a sharp two-hour discussion. The focus on just four elements generated a clear picture of the project's strengths and weaknesses. For instance, managers learned that the restructuring would take eight months to implement but that it had poorly defined milestones and reviews. Although the project team was capable and senior management showed reasonable commitment to the effort, there was room for improvement in both areas. The back-office workforce was hostile to the proposed changes since more than 20% of these people would lose their jobs. Managers and employees agreed that the back-office staff would need to muster 10% to 20% more effort on top of its existing commitments during the implementation. On the DICE scale, the project was deep in the Woe Zone.

However, the assessment also led managers to take steps to increase the possibility of success before they started the project. The bank decided to split the project time line into two—one short-term and one long-term. Doing so allowed the bank to schedule review points more frequently and to maximize team members' ability to learn from experience before the transformation grew in complexity. To improve staff commitment, the bank decided to devote more time to explaining why the change was necessary and how the institution would support the staff during the implementation. The bank also took a closer look at the people who would be involved in the project and changed some of the team leaders when it realized that they lacked the necessary skills. Finally, senior managers made a concerted effort to show their backing for the initiative by holding a traveling road show to explain the project to people at all levels of the organization. Taken together, the bank's actions and plans shifted the project into the Win Zone. Fourteen months later, the bank completed the project—on time and below budget.

Applying the DICE Framework

The simplicity of the DICE framework often proves to be its biggest problem; executives seem to desire more complex answers. By overlooking the obvious, however, they often end up making compromises that don't work. Smart companies try to ensure that they don't fall into that trap by using the DICE framework in one of three ways.

Track Projects

Some companies train managers in how to use the DICE framework before they start transformation programs. Executives use spreadsheet-based versions of the tool to calculate the DICE scores of the various components of the program and to compare them with past scores. Over time, every score must be balanced against the trajectory of scores and, as we shall see next, the portfolio of scores.

Senior executives often use DICE assessments as early warning indicators that transformation initiatives are in trouble. That's how Amgen, the $10.6 billion biotechnology company, used the DICE framework. In 2001, the company realigned its operations around some key processes, broadened its offerings, relaunched some mature products, allied with some firms and acquired others, and launched several innovations. To avoid implementation problems, Amgen's top management team used the DICE framework to gauge how effectively it had allocated people, senior management time, and other resources. As soon as projects reported troubling scores, designated executives paid attention to them. They reviewed the projects more often, reconfigured the teams, and allocated more resources to them. In one area of the change project, Amgen used DICE to track 300 initiatives and reconfigured 200 of them.

Both big and small organizations can put the tool to good use. Take the case of a hospital that kicked off six change projects in the late 1990s. Each initiative involved a lot of investment, had significant clinical implications, or both. The hospital's general manager felt that some projects were going well but was concerned about others. He wasn't able to attribute his concerns to anything other than a bad feeling. However, when the general manager used the DICE framework, he was able to confirm his suspicions. After a 45-minute discussion with project managers and other key people, he established that three projects were in the Win Zone but two were in the Woe Zone and one was in the Worry Zone.

The strongest projects, the general manager found, consumed more than their fair share of resources. Senior hospital staff sensed that those projects would succeed and spent more time promoting them, attending meetings about them, and making sure they had sufficient resources. By contrast, no one enjoyed attending meetings on projects that were performing poorly. So the general manager stopped attending meetings for the projects that were on track; he attended only sessions that related to the three underperforming ones. He pulled some managers from the projects that were progressing smoothly and moved them to the riskier efforts. He added more milestones to the struggling enterprises, delayed their completion, and pushed hard for improvement. Those steps helped ensure that all six projects met their objectives.

Manage portfolios of projects

When companies launch large transformation programs, they kick off many projects to attain their objectives. But if executives don't manage the portfolio properly, those tasks end up competing for attention and resources. For instance, senior executives may choose the best employees for projects they have sponsored or lavish attention on pet projects rather than on those that need attention. By deploying our framework before they start transformation initiatives, companies can identify problem projects in portfolios, focus execution expertise and senior management attention where it is most needed, and defuse political issues.

Take, for example, the case of an Australasian manufacturing company that had planned a set of 40 projects as part of a program to improve profitability. Since some had greater financial implications than others, the company's general manager called for a meeting with all the project owners and senior managers. The group went through each project, debating its DICE score and identifying the problem areas. After listing all the scores and issues, the general manager walked to a whiteboard and circled the five most important projects. "I'm prepared to accept that some projects will start off in the Worry Zone, though I won't accept anything outside the middle of this zone for more than a few weeks. For the top five, we're not going to start until these are well within the Win Zone. What do we have to do to achieve that?" he asked.

The group began thinking and acting right away. It moved people around on teams, reconfigured some projects, and identified those that senior managers should pay more attention to—all of which helped raise DICE scores before implementation began. The most important projects were set up for resounding success while most of the remaining ones managed to get into the Win Zone. The group left some projects in the Worry Zone, but it agreed to track them closely to ensure that their scores improved. In our experience, that's the right thing to do. When companies are trying to overhaul themselves, they shouldn't have all their projects in the Win Zone; if they do, they are not ambitious enough. Transformations should entail fundamental changes that stretch an organization.

Force conversation

When different executives calculate DICE scores for the same project, the results can vary widely. The difference in scores is particularly important in terms of the dialogue it triggers. It provokes participants and engages them in debate over questions like "Why do we see the project in these different ways?" and "What can we agree to do to ensure that the project will succeed?" That's critical, because even people within the same organization lack a common framework for discussing problems with change initiatives. Prejudices, differences in perspectives, and a reluctance or inability to speak up can block effective debates. By using the DICE framework, companies can create a common language and force the right discussions.

Sometimes, companies hold workshops to review floundering projects. At those two- to four-hour sessions, groups of eight to 15 senior and middle managers, along with the project team and the project sponsors, hold a candid dialogue. The debate usually moves beyond the project's scores to the underlying causes of problems and possible remedies. The workshops bring diverse opinions to light, which often can be combined into innovative solutions. Consider, for example, the manner in which DICE workshops helped a telecommunications service provider that had planned a major transformation effort. Consisting of five strategic initiatives and 50 subprojects that needed to be up and running quickly, the program confronted some serious obstacles. The projects' goals, time lines, and revenue objectives were unclear. There were delays in approving business cases, a dearth of rigor and focus in planning and identifying milestones, and a shortage of resources. There were leadership issues, too. For example, executive-level shortcomings had resulted in poor coordination of projects and a misjudgment of risks.

To put the transformation program on track, the telecom company incorporated DICE into project managers' tool kits. The Project Management Office arranged a series of workshops to analyze issues and decide future steps. One workshop, for example, was devoted to three new product development projects, two of which had landed in the Woe Zone and one in the Worry Zone. Participants traced the problems to tension between managers and technology experts, underfunding, lack of manpower, and poor definition of the projects' scopes. They eventually agreed on three remedial actions: holding a conflict-resolution meeting between the directors in charge of technology and those responsible for the core business; making sure senior leadership paid immediate attention to the resource issues; and bringing together the project team and the line-of-business head to formalize project objectives. With the project sponsor committed to those actions, the three projects had improved their DICE scores and thus their chances of success at the time this article went to press.

Conversations about DICE scores are particularly useful for large-scale transformations that cut across business units, functions, and locations. In such change efforts, it is critical to find the right balance between centralized oversight, which ensures that everyone in the organization takes the effort seriously and understands the goals, and the autonomy that various initiatives need. Teams must have the flexibility and incentive to produce customized solutions for their markets, functions, and competitive environments. The balance is difficult to achieve without an explicit consideration of the DICE variables.

Take the case of a leading global beverage company that needed to increase operational efficiency and focus on the most promising brands and markets. The company also sought to make key processes such as consumer demand development and customer fulfillment more innovative. The CEO's goals were ambitious and required investing significant resources across the company. Top management faced enormous challenges in structuring the effort and in spawning projects that focused on the right issues. Executives knew that this was a multiyear effort, yet without tight schedules and oversight of individual projects, there was a risk that projects would take far too long to be completed and the results would taper off.

To mitigate the risks, senior managers decided to analyze each project at several levels of the organization. Using the DICE framework, they reviewed each effort every month until they felt confident that it was on track. After that, reviews occurred when projects met major milestones. No more than two months elapsed between reviews, even in the later stages of the program. The time between reviews at the project-team level was even shorter: Team leaders reviewed progress biweekly throughout the transformation. Some of the best people joined the effort full time. The human resources department took an active role in recruiting team members, thereby creating a virtuous cycle in which the best people began to seek involvement in various initiatives. During the course of the transformation, the company promoted several team members to line- and functional leadership positions because of their performance.

The company's change program resulted in hundreds of millions of dollars of value creation. Its once-stagnant brands began to grow, it cracked open new markets such as China, and sales and promotion activities were aligned with the fastest-growing channels. There were many moments during the process when inertia in the organization threatened to derail the change efforts. However, senior management's belief in focusing on the four key variables helped move the company to a higher trajectory of performance.

By providing a common language for change, the DICE framework allows companies to tap into the insight and experience of their employees. A great deal has been said about middle managers who want to block change. We find that most middle managers are prepared to support change efforts even if doing so involves additional work and uncertainty and puts their jobs at risk. However, they resist change because they don't have sufficient input in shaping those initiatives. Too often, they lack the tools, the language, and the forums in which to express legitimate concerns about the design and implementation of change projects. That's where a standard, quantitative, and simple framework comes in. By enabling frank conversations at all levels within organizations, the DICE framework helps people do the right thing by change.

Originally published in October 2005. Reprint R0510G

Why Change Programs Don't Produce Change

by Michael Beer, Russell A. Eisenstat, and Bert Spector

IN THE MID-1980S, THE NEW CEO of a major international bank—call it U.S. Financial—announced a companywide change effort. Deregulation was posing serious competitive challenges—challenges to which the bank's traditional hierarchical organization was ill-suited to respond. The only solution was to change fundamentally how the company operated. And the place to begin was at the top.

The CEO held a retreat with his top 15 executives where they painstakingly reviewed the bank's purpose and culture. He published a mission statement and hired a new vice president for human resources from a company well-known for its excellence in managing people. And in a quick succession of moves, he established companywide programs to push change down through the organization: a new organizational structure, a performance appraisal system, a pay-for-performance compensation plan, training programs to turn managers into "change agents," and quarterly attitude surveys to chart the progress of the change effort.

As much as these steps sound like a textbook case in organizational transformation, there was one big problem: two years after the CEO launched the change program, virtually nothing in the way of actual changes in organizational behavior had occurred. What had gone wrong?

The answer is "everything." Every one of the assumptions the CEO made—about who should lead the change effort, what needed changing, and how to go about doing it—was wrong.

U.S. Financial's story reflects a common problem. Faced with changing markets and increased competition, more and more companies are struggling to reestablish their dominance, regain market share, and in some cases, ensure their survival. Many have come to understand that the key to competitive success is to transform the way they function. They are reducing reliance on managerial authority, formal rules and procedures, and narrow divisions of work. And they are creating teams, sharing information, and delegating responsibility and accountability far down the hierarchy. In effect, companies are moving from the hierarchical and bureaucratic model of organization that has characterized corporations since World War II to what we call the task-driven organization where what has to be done governs who works with whom and who leads.

But while senior managers understand the necessity of change to cope with new competitive realities, they often misunderstand what it takes to bring it about. They tend to share two assumptions with the CEO of U.S. Financial: that promulgating companywide programs—mission statements, "corporate culture" programs, training courses, quality circles, and new pay-for-performance systems—will transform organizations, and that employee behavior is changed by altering a company's formal structure and systems.

In a four-year study of organizational change at six large corporations (see the sidebar, "Tracking Corporate Change"; the names are fictitious), we found that exactly the opposite is true: the greatest obstacle to revitalization is the idea that it comes about through companywide change programs, particularly when a corporate staff group such as human resources sponsors them. We call this "the fallacy of programmatic change." Just as important, formal organization structure and systems cannot lead a corporate renewal process.

While in some companies, wave after wave of programs rolled across the landscape with little positive impact, in others, more successful transformations did take place. They usually started at the periphery of the corporation in a few plants and divisions far from

Idea in Brief

Two years after launching a change program to counter competitive threats, a bank CEO realized his effort had produced . . . no change. Surprising, since he and his top executives had reviewed the company's purpose and culture, published a mission statement, and launched programs (e.g., pay for-performance compensation) designed to push change throughout the organization.

But revitalization doesn't come from the top. It starts at an organization's periphery, led by unit managers creating ad hoc arrangements to solve concrete problems. Through **task alignment**—directing employees' responsibilities and relationships toward the company's central competitive task—these managers focus energy on *work*, not abstractions like "empowerment" or "culture."

Senior managers' role in this process? Specify the company's desired *general* direction, without dictating solutions. Then spread the lessons of revitalized units throughout the company.

corporate headquarters. And they were led by the general managers of those units, not by the CEO or corporate staff people.

The general managers did not focus on formal structures and systems; they created ad hoc organizational arrangements to solve concrete business problems. By aligning employee roles, responsibilities, and relationships to address the organization's most important competitive task—a process we call "task alignment"—they focused energy for change on the work itself, not on abstractions such as "participation" or "culture." Unlike the CEO at U.S. Financial, they didn't employ massive training programs or rely on speeches and mission statements. Instead, we saw that general managers carefully developed the change process through a sequence of six basic managerial interventions.

Once general managers understand the logic of this sequence, they don't have to wait for senior management to start a process of organizational revitalization. There is a lot they can do even without support from the top. Of course, having a CEO or other senior managers who are committed to change does make a difference—and when it comes to changing an entire organization, such support is

Idea in Practice

Successful change requires commitment, coordination, and competency.

1. Mobilize commitment to change through joint diagnosis of problems

Example: Navigation Devices had never made a profit or high-quality, cost-competitive product—because top-down decisions ignored cross-functional coordination.To change this,a new general manager had his *entire* team broadly assess the business. Then, his task force of engineers, production workers, managers, and union officials visited successful manufacturing organizations to identify improvement ideas. One plant's *team* approach impressed them, illuminated their own problem, and suggested a solution. Commitment to change intensified.

2. Develop a shared vision of how to organize for competitiveness

Remove functional and hierarchical barriers to information sharing and problem solving—by changing roles and responsibilities, not titles or compensation.

Example: Navigation's task force proposed developing products through cross-functional teams. A larger team refined this model and presented it to all employees—who supported it because it stemmed from their own analysis of their business problems.

3. Foster consensus for the new vision, competence to enact it, and cohesion to advance it

This requires the general manager's strong leadership.

essential. But top management's role in the change process is very different from that which the CEO played at U.S. Financial.

Grass-roots change presents senior managers with a paradox: directing a "nondirective" change process. The most effective senior managers in our study recognized their limited power to mandate corporate renewal from the top. Instead, they defined their roles as creating a climate for change, then spreading the lessons of both successes and failures. Put another way, they specified the general direction in which the company should move without insisting on specific solutions.

In the early phases of a companywide change process, any senior manager can play this role. Once grass-roots change reaches a critical mass, however, the CEO has to be ready to transform his or her

Example: Navigation's general manager fostered *consensus* by supporting those who were committed to change and offering outplacement and counseling to those who weren't; *competence* by providing requested training; and *cohesion* by redeploying managers who couldn't function in the new organization. Change accelerated.

4. Spread revitalization to all departments—without pushing from the top

Example: Navigation's new team structure required engineers to collaborate with production workers. Encouraged to develop their own approach to teamwork and coordination, the engineers selected matrix management. People willingly learned needed skills and attitudes, because the new structure was *their* choice.

5. Institutionalize revitalization through formal policies, systems, and structures . . . only *after* your new approach is up and running.

Example: Navigation boosted its profits—without changing reporting relationships, evaluation procedures, or compensation. Only then did the general manager alter formal structures; e.g., eliminating a VP so that engineering and manufacturing reported directly to him.

6. Monitor the revitalization process, adjusting in response to problems

Example: At Navigation, an oversight team of managers, a union leader, an engineer, and a financial analyst kept watch over the change process—continually learning, adapting, and strengthening the commitment to change.

own work unit as well—the top team composed of key business heads and corporate staff heads. At this point, the company's structure and systems must be put into alignment with the new management practices that have developed at the periphery. Otherwise, the tension between dynamic units and static top management will cause the change process to break down.

We believe that an approach to change based on task alignment, starting at the periphery and moving steadily toward the corporate core, is the most effective way to achieve enduring organizational change. This is not to say that change can never start at the top, but it is uncommon and too risky as a deliberate strategy. Change is about learning. It is a rare CEO who knows in advance the fine-grained details of organizational change that the many diverse units of a large corporation demand. Moreover, most of today's senior executives developed in an era in which top-down hierarchy was the primary means for organizing and managing. They must learn from innovative approaches coming from younger unit managers closer to the action.

The Fallacy of Programmatic Change

Most change programs don't work because they are guided by a theory of change that is fundamentally flawed. The common belief is that the place to begin is with the knowledge and attitudes of individuals. Changes in attitudes, the theory goes, lead to changes in individual behavior. And changes in individual behavior, repeated by many people, will result in organizational change. According to this model, change is like a conversion experience. Once people "get religion," changes in their behavior will surely follow.

This theory gets the change process exactly backward. In fact, individual behavior is powerfully shaped by the organizational roles that people play. The most effective way to change behavior, therefore, is to put people into a new organizational context, which imposes new roles, responsibilities, and relationships on them. This creates a situation that, in a sense, "forces" new attitudes and behaviors on people. (See the table, "Contrasting assumptions about change.")

One way to think about this challenge is in terms of three interrelated factors required for corporate revitalization. *Coordination* or teamwork is especially important if an organization is to discover and act on cost, quality, and product development opportunities. The production and sale of innovative, high-quality, low-cost products (or services) depend on close coordination among marketing, product design, and manufacturing departments, as well as between labor and management. High levels of *commitment* are essential for the effort, initiative, and cooperation that coordinated action demands. New *competencies* such as knowledge of the business as a whole, analytical skills, and interpersonal skills are necessary if people are to identify and solve problems as a team. If any of these elements are missing, the change process will break down.

Tracking Corporate Change

WHICH STRATEGIES FOR CORPORATE change work, and which do not? We sought the answers in a comprehensive study of 12 large companies where top management was attempting to revitalize the corporation. Based on preliminary research, we identified 6 for in-depth analysis: 5 manufacturing companies and 1 large international bank. All had revenues between $4 billion and $10 billion. We studied 26 plants and divisions in these 6 companies and conducted hundreds of interviews with human resource managers; line managers engaged in change efforts at plants, branches, or business units; workers and union leaders; and, finally, top management.

Based on this material, we ranked the 6 companies according to the success with which they had managed the revitalization effort. Were there significant improvements in interfunctional coordination, decision making, work organizations, and concern for people? Research has shown that in the long term, the quality of these 4 factors will influence performance. We did not define success in terms of improved financial performance because, in the short run, corporate financial performance is influenced by many situational factors unrelated to the change process.

To corroborate our rankings of the companies, we also administered a standardized questionnaire in each company to understand how employers viewed the unfolding change process. Respondents rated their companies on a scale of 1 to 5. A score of 3 meant that no change had taken place; a score below 3 meant that, in the employee's judgment, the organization had actually gotten worse. As the table suggests, with one exception—the company we call Livingston Electronics—employees' perceptions of how much their

Researchers and employees—similar conclusions

Extent of revitalization

Company	Ranked by researchers	Rated by employees	
		Average	*Standard deviation*
General Products	1	4.04	.35
Fairweather	2	3.58	.45
Livingston Electronics	3	3.61	.76
Scranton Steel	4	3.30	.65
Continental Glass	5	2.96	.83
U.S. Financial	6	2.78	1.07

Tracking Corporate Change (continued)

companies had changed were identical to ours. And Livingston's relatively high standard of deviation (which measures the degree of consensus among employees about the outcome of the change effort) indicates that within the company there was considerable disagreement as to just how successful revitalization had been.

The problem with most companywide change programs is that they address only one or, at best, two of these factors. Just because a company issues a philosophy statement about teamwork doesn't mean its employees necessarily know what teams to form or how to function within them to improve coordination. A corporate reorganization may change the boxes on a formal organization chart but not provide the necessary attitudes and skills to make the new structure work. A pay-for-performance system may force managers to differentiate better performers from poorer ones, but it doesn't help them internalize new standards by which to judge subordinates' performances. Nor does it teach them how to deal effectively with

---

Contrasting assumptions about change

Programmatic change	Task alignment
Problems in behavior are a function of individual knowledge, attitudes, and beliefs.	Individual knowledge, attitudes and beliefs are shaped by recurring patterns of behavioral interactions.
The primary target of renewal should be the content of attitudes and ideas; actual behavior should be secondary.	The primary target of renewal should be behavior; attitudes and ideas should be secondary.
Behavior can be isolated and changed individually.	Problems in behavior come from a circular pattern, but the effects of the organizational system on the individual are greater than those of the individual on the system.
The target for renewal should be at the individual level.	The target for renewal should be at the level of roles, responsibilities, and relationships.

performance problems. Such programs cannot provide the cultural context (role models from whom to learn) that people need to develop new competencies, so ultimately they fail to create organizational change.

Similarly, training programs may target competence, but rarely do they change a company's patterns of coordination. Indeed, the excitement engendered in a good corporate training program frequently leads to increased frustration when employees get back on the job only to see their new skills go unused in an organization in which nothing else has changed. People end up seeing training as a waste of time, which undermines whatever commitment to change a program may have roused in the first place.

When one program doesn't work, senior managers, like the CEO at U.S. Financial, often try another, instituting a rapid progression of programs. But this only exacerbates the problem. Because they are designed to cover everyone and everything, programs end up covering nobody and nothing particularly well. They are so general and standardized that they don't speak to the day-to-day realities of particular units. Buzzwords like "quality," "participation," "excellence," "empowerment," and "leadership" become a substitute for a detailed understanding of the business.

And all these change programs also undermine the credibility of the change effort. Even when managers accept the potential value of a particular program for others—quality circles, for example, to solve a manufacturing problem—they may be confronted with another, more pressing business problem such as new product development. One-size-fits-all change programs take energy *away* from efforts to solve key business problems—which explains why so many general managers don't support programs, even when they acknowledge that their underlying principles may be useful.

This is not to state that training, changes in pay systems or organizational structure, or a new corporate philosophy are always inappropriate. All can play valuable roles in supporting an integrated change effort. The problems come when such programs are used in isolation as a kind of "magic bullet" to spread organizational change rapidly through the entire corporation. At their best, change programs of this sort are irrelevant. At their worst, they actually inhibit change. By promoting skepticism and cynicism, programmatic change can inoculate companies against the real thing.

Six Steps to Effective Change

Companies avoid the shortcomings of programmatic change by concentrating on "task alignment"—reorganizing employee roles, responsibilities, and relationships to solve specific business problems. Task alignment is easiest in small units—a plant, department, or business unit—where goals and tasks are clearly defined. Thus the chief problem for corporate change is how to promote task-aligned change across many diverse units.

We saw that general managers at the business unit or plant level can achieve task alignment through a sequence of six overlapping but distinctive steps, which we call the *critical path*. This path develops a self-reinforcing cycle of commitment, coordination, and competence. The sequence of steps is important because activities appropriate at one time are often counterproductive if started too early. Timing is everything in the management of change.

1. Mobilize commitment to change through joint diagnosis of business problems. As the term task alignment suggests, the starting point of any effective change effort is a clearly defined business problem. By helping people develop a shared diagnosis of what is wrong in an organization and what can and must be improved, a general manager mobilizes the initial commitment that is necessary to begin the change process.

Consider the case of a division we call Navigation Devices, a business unit of about 600 people set up by a large corporation to commercialize a product originally designed for the military market. When the new general manager took over, the division had been in operation for several years without ever making a profit. It had never been able to design and produce a high-quality, cost-competitive product. This was due largely to an organization in which decisions were made at the top, without proper involvement of or coordination with other functions.

The first step the new general manager took was to initiate a broad review of the business. Where the previous general manager had set strategy with the unit's marketing director alone, the new general manager included his entire management team. He also brought in outside consultants to help him and his managers function more effectively as a group.

Next, he formed a 20-person task force representing all the stakeholders in the organization—managers, engineers, production workers, and union officials. The group visited a number of successful manufacturing organizations in an attempt to identify what Navigation Devices might do to organize more effectively. One high-performance manufacturing plant in the task force's own company made a particularly strong impression. Not only did it highlight the problems at Navigation Devices but it also offered an alternative organizational model, based on teams, that captured the group's imagination. Seeing a different way of working helped strengthen the group's commitment to change.

The Navigation Devices task force didn't learn new facts from this process of joint diagnosis; everyone already knew the unit was losing money. But the group came to see clearly the organizational roots of the unit's inability to compete and, even more important, came to share a common understanding of the problem. The group also identified a potential organizational solution: to redesign the way it worked, using ad hoc teams to integrate the organization around the competitive task.

2. Develop a shared vision of how to organize and manage for competitiveness. Once a core group of people is committed to a particular analysis of the problem, the general manager can lead employees toward a task-aligned vision of the organization that defines new roles and responsibilities. These new arrangements will coordinate the flow of information and work across interdependent functions at all levels of the organization. But since they do not change formal structures and systems like titles or compensation, they encounter less resistance.

At Navigation Devices, the 20-person task force became the vehicle for this second stage. The group came up with a model of the organization in which cross-functional teams would accomplish all work, particularly new product development. A business-management team composed of the general manager and his staff would set the unit's strategic direction and review the work of lower level teams. Business-area teams would develop plans for specific markets. Product-development teams would manage new products from initial design to production. Production-process teams composed of engineers and production workers would identify and solve quality and cost problems in the plant. Finally, engineering-process teams would examine engineering methods and equipment. The teams got to the root of the unit's problems—functional and hierarchical barriers to sharing information and solving problems.

To create a consensus around the new vision, the general manager commissioned a still larger task force of about 90 employees from different levels and functions, including union and management, to refine the vision and obtain everyone's commitment to it. On a retreat away from the workplace, the group further refined the new organizational model and drafted a values statement, which it presented later to the entire Navigation Devices work force. The vision and the values statement made sense to Navigation Devices employees in a way many corporate mission statements never do—because it grew out of the organization's own analysis of real business problems. And it was built on a model for solving those problems that key stakeholders believed would work.

3. Foster consensus for the new vision, competence to enact it, and cohesion to move it along. Simply letting employees help develop a new vision is not enough to overcome resistance to change—or to foster the skills needed to make the new organization work. Not everyone can help in the design, and even those who do participate often do not fully appreciate what renewal will require until the new organization is actually in place. This is when strong leadership from the general manager is crucial. Commitment to change is always uneven. Some managers are enthusiastic; others are neutral or even antagonistic. At Navigation Devices, the general manager used what his subordinates termed the "velvet glove." He made it clear that the division was going to encourage employee involvement and the team approach. To managers who wanted to help him, he offered support. To those who did not, he offered outplacement and counseling.

Once an organization has defined new roles and responsibilities, people need to develop the competencies to make the new setup work. Actually, the very existence of the teams with their new goals and accountabilities will force learning. The changes in roles, responsibilities, and relationships foster new skills and attitudes. Changed patterns of coordination will also increase employee participation, collaboration, and information sharing.

But management also has to provide the right supports. At Navigation Devices, six resource people—three from the unit's human resource department and three from corporate headquarters—worked on the change project. Each team was assigned one internal consultant, who attended every meeting, to help people be effective team members. Once employees could see exactly what kinds of new skills they needed, they asked for formal training programs to develop those skills further. Since these courses grew directly out of the employees' own experiences, they were far more focused and useful than traditional training programs.

Some people, of course, just cannot or will not change, despite all the direction and support in the world. Step three is the appropriate time to replace those managers who cannot function in the new organization—after they have had a chance to prove themselves. Such decisions are rarely easy, and sometimes those people who have difficulty working in a participatory organization have extremely valuable specialized skills. Replacing them early in the change process, before they have worked in the new organization, is not only unfair to individuals; it can be demoralizing to the entire organization and can disrupt the change process. People's understanding of what kind of manager and worker the new organization demands grows slowly and only from the experience of seeing some individuals succeed and others fail.

Once employees have bought into a vision of what's necessary and have some understanding of what the new organization requires, they can accept the necessity of replacing or moving people who don't make the transition to the new way of working. Sometimes people are transferred to other parts of the company where technical expertise rather than the new competencies is the main requirement. When no alternatives exist, sometimes they leave the company through early retirement programs, for example. The act of replacing people can actually reinforce the organization's commitment to change by visibly demonstrating the general manager's commitment to the new way.

Some of the managers replaced at Navigation Devices were high up in the organization—for example, the vice president of operations, who oversaw the engineering and manufacturing departments. The new head of manufacturing was far more committed to change and skilled in leading a critical path change process. The result was speedier change throughout the manufacturing function.

4. Spread revitalization to all departments without pushing it from the top. With the new ad hoc organization for the unit in place, it is time to turn to the functional and staff departments that must interact with it. Members of teams cannot be effective unless the department from which they come is organized and managed in a way that supports their roles as full-fledged participants in team decisions. What this often means is that these departments will have to rethink their roles and authority in the organization.

At Navigation Devices, this process was seen most clearly in the engineering department. Production department managers were the most enthusiastic about the change effort; engineering managers were more hesitant. Engineering had always been king at Navigation Devices; engineers designed products to the military's specifications without much concern about whether manufacturing could easily build them or not. Once the new team structure was in place, however, engineers had to participate on product-development teams with production workers. This required them to re-examine their roles and rethink their approaches to organizing and managing their own department.

The impulse of many general managers faced with such a situation would be to force the issue—to announce, for example, that now all parts of the organization must manage by teams. The temptation to force newfound insights on the rest of the organization can be great, particularly when rapid change is needed, but it would be the same mistake that senior managers make when they try to push programmatic change throughout a company. It short-circuits the change process.

It's better to let each department "reinvent the wheel"—that is, to find its own way to the new organization. At Navigation Devices, each department was allowed to take the general concepts of coordination and teamwork and apply them to its particular situation. Engineering spent nearly a year agonizing over how to implement the team concept. The department conducted two surveys, held off-site meetings, and proposed, rejected, then accepted a matrix management structure before it finally got on board. Engineering's decision to move to matrix management was not surprising, but because it was its own choice, people committed themselves to learning the necessary new skills and attitudes.

5. Institutionalize revitalization through formal policies, systems, and structures. There comes a point where general managers have to consider how to institutionalize change so that the process continues even after they've moved on to other responsibilities. Step five is the time: the new approach has become entrenched, the right people are in place, and the team organization is up and running. Enacting changes in structures and systems any earlier tends to backfire. Take information systems. Creating a team structure means new information requirements. Why not have the MIS department create new systems that cut across traditional functional and departmental lines early in the change process? The problem is that without a well-developed understanding of information requirements, which can best be obtained by placing people on task-aligned teams, managers are likely to resist new systems as an imposition by the MIS department. Newly formed teams can often pull together enough information to get their work done without fancy new systems. It's better to hold off until everyone understands what the team's information needs are.

What's true for information systems is even more true for other formal structures and systems. Any formal system is going to have some disadvantages; none is perfect. These imperfections can be minimized, however, once people have worked in an ad hoc team structure and learned what interdependencies are necessary. Then employees will commit to them too.

Again, Navigation Devices is a good example. The revitalization of the unit was highly successful. Employees changed how they saw their roles and responsibilities and became convinced that change could actually make a difference. As a result, there were dramatic improvements in value added per employee, scrap reduction, quality, customer service, gross inventory per employee, and profits. And all this happened with almost no formal changes in reporting relationships, information systems, evaluation procedures, compensation, or control systems.

When the opportunity arose, the general manager eventually did make some changes in the formal organization. For example, when he moved the vice president of operations out of the organization, he eliminated the position altogether. Engineering and manufacturing reported directly to him from that point on. For the most part, however, the changes in performance at Navigation Devices were sustained by the general manager's expectations and the new norms for behavior.

6. Monitor and adjust strategies in response to problems in the revitalization process. The purpose of change is to create an asset that did not exist before—a learning organization capable of adapting to a changing competitive environment. The organization has to know how to continually monitor its behavior—in effect, to learn how to learn.

Some might say that this is the general manager's responsibility. But monitoring the change process needs to be shared, just as analyzing the organization's key business problem does.

At Navigation Devices, the general manager introduced several mechanisms to allow key constituents to help monitor the revitalization. An oversight team—composed of some crucial managers, a union leader, a secretary, an engineer, and an analyst from finance—kept continual watch over the process. Regular employee attitude surveys monitored behavior patterns. Planning teams were formed and reformed in response to new challenges. All these mechanisms created a long-term capacity for continual adaptation and learning.

The six-step process provides a way to elicit renewal without imposing it. When stakeholders become committed to a vision, they are willing to accept a new pattern of management—here the ad hoc team structure—that demands changes in their behavior. And as the employees discover that the new approach is more effective (which will happen only if the vision aligns with the core task), they have to grapple with personal and organizational changes they might otherwise resist. Finally, as improved coordination helps solve relevant problems, it will reinforce team behavior and produce a desire to learn new skills. This learning enhances effectiveness even further and results in an even stronger commitment to change. This mutually reinforcing cycle of improvements in commitment, coordination, and competence creates a growing sense of efficacy. It can continue as long as the ad hoc team structure is allowed to expand its role in running the business.

The Role of Top Management

To change an entire corporation, the change process we have described must be applied over and over again in many plants, branches, departments, and divisions. Orchestrating this company-wide change process is the first responsibility of senior management. Doing so successfully requires a delicate balance. Without explicit efforts by top management to promote conditions for change in individual units, only a few plants or divisions will attempt change, and those that do will remain isolated. The best senior manager leaders we studied held their subordinates responsible for starting a change process without specifying a particular approach.

Create a market for change. The most effective approach is to set demanding standards for all operations and then hold managers accountable to them. At our best-practice company, which we call General Products, senior managers developed ambitious product and operating standards. General managers unable to meet these product standards by a certain date had to scrap their products and take a sharp hit to their bottom lines. As long as managers understand that high standards are not arbitrary but are dictated by competitive forces, standards can generate enormous pressure for better performance, a key ingredient in mobilizing energy for change.

But merely increasing demands is not enough. Under pressure, most managers will seek to improve business performance by doing more of what they have always done—overmanage—rather than alter the fundamental way they organize. So, while senior managers increase demands, they should also hold managers accountable for fundamental changes in the way they use human resources.

For example, when plant managers at General Products complained about the impossibility of meeting new business standards, senior managers pointed them to the corporate organization-development department within human resources and emphasized that the plant managers would be held accountable for moving revitalization along. Thus top management had created a demand system for help with the new way of managing, and the human resource staff could support change without appearing to push a program.

Use successfully revitalized units as organizational models for the entire company. Another important strategy is to focus the company's attention on plants and divisions that have already begun experimenting with management innovations. These units become developmental laboratories for further innovation.

There are two ground rules for identifying such models. First, innovative units need support. They need the best managers to lead them, and they need adequate resources—for instance, skilled human resource people and external consultants. In the most successful companies that we studied, senior managers saw it as their responsibility to make resources available to leading-edge units. They did not leave it to the human resource function.

Second, because resources are always limited and the costs of failure high, it is crucial to identify those units with the likeliest chance of success. Successful management innovations can appear to be failures when the bottom line is devastated by environmental factors beyond the unit's control. The best models are in healthy markets.

Obviously, organizational models can serve as catalysts for change only if others are aware of their existence and are encouraged to learn from them. Many of our worst-practice companies had plants and divisions that were making substantial changes. The problem was, nobody knew about them. Corporate management had never bothered to highlight them as examples to follow. In the leading companies, visits, conferences, and educational programs facilitated learning from model units.

Develop career paths that encourage leadership development. Without strong leaders, units cannot make the necessary organizational changes, yet the scarcest resource available for revitalizing corporations is leadership. Corporate renewal depends as much on developing effective change leaders as it does on developing effective organizations. The personal learning associated with leadership development—or the realization by higher management that a manager does not have this capacity—cannot occur in the classroom. It only happens in an organization where the teamwork, high commitment, and new competencies we have discussed are already the norm.

The only way to develop the kind of leaders a changing organization needs is to make leadership an important criterion for promotion, and then manage people's careers to develop it. At our best-practice companies, managers were moved from job to job and from organization to organization based on their learning needs, not on their position in the hierarchy. Successful leaders were assigned to units that had been targeted for change. People who needed to sharpen their leadership skills were moved into the company's model units where those skills would be demanded and therefore learned. In effect, top management used leading-edge units as hothouses to develop revitalization leaders.

But what about the top management team itself? How important is it for the CEO and his or her direct reports to practice what they preach? It is not surprising—indeed, it's predictable—that in the early years of a corporate change effort, top managers' actions are often not consistent with their words. Such inconsistencies don't pose a major barrier to corporate change in the beginning, though consistency is obviously desirable. Senior managers can create a climate for grass-roots change without paying much attention to how they themselves operate and manage. And unit managers will tolerate this inconsistency so long as they can freely make changes in their own units in order to compete more effectively.

There comes a point, however, when addressing the inconsistencies becomes crucial. As the change process spreads, general managers in the ever-growing circle of revitalized units eventually demand changes from corporate staff groups and top management. As they discover how to manage differently in their own units, they bump up against constraints of policies and practices that corporate staff and top management have created. They also begin to see opportunities for better coordination between themselves and other parts of the company over which they have little control. At this point, corporate organization must be aligned with corporate strategy, and coordination between related but hitherto independent businesses improved for the benefit of the whole corporation.

None of the companies we studied had reached this "moment of truth." Even when corporate leaders intellectually understood the direction of change, they were just beginning to struggle with how they would change themselves and the company as a whole for a total corporate revitalization.

This last step in the process of corporate renewal is probably the most important. If the CEO and his or her management team do not ultimately apply to themselves what they have been encouraging their general managers to do, then the whole process can break down. The time to tackle the tough challenge of transforming companywide systems and structures comes finally at the end of the corporate change process.

At this point, senior managers must make an effort to adopt the team behavior, attitudes, and skills that they have demanded of others in earlier phases of change. Their struggle with behavior change will help sustain corporate renewal in three ways. It will promote the attitudes and behavior needed to coordinate diverse activities in the company; it will lend credibility to top management's continued espousal of change; and it will help the CEO identify and develop a successor who is capable of learning the new behaviors. Only such a manager can lead a corporation that can renew itself continually as competitive forces change.

Companies need a particular mind-set for managing change: one that emphasizes process over specific content, recognizes organization change as a unit-by-unit learning process rather than a series of programs, and acknowledges the payoffs that result from persistence over a long period of time as opposed to quick fixes. This mind-set is difficult to maintain in an environment that presses for quarterly earnings, but we believe it is the only approach that will bring about successful renewal.

Originally published in November 1990. Reprint 90601

About the Contributors

MICHAEL BEER is the Cahners-Rabb Professor of Business Administration, Emeritus, at Harvard Business School.

RUSSELL A. EISENSTAT is a partner at TruePoint, a management consulting firm in Massachusetts, and a former professor at Harvard Business School.

DAVID A. GARVIN is the C. Roland Christensen Professor of Business Administration at Harvard Business School.

RONALD A. HEIFETZ codirects the Center for Public Leadership at Harvard University's Kennedy School of Government.

PAUL HEMP, formerly a senior editor of *Harvard Business Review,* is the global director of brand transformation at HCL Technologies.

ALAN JACKSON is a senior partner at The Boston Consulting Group.

PERRY KEENAN is a partner and managing director in The Boston Consulting Group's Chicago office.

ROBERT KEGAN is the William and Miriam Meehan Professor in Adult Learning and Professional Development at Harvard's Graduate School of Education.

W. CHAN KIM is the Boston Consulting Group Bruce D. Henderson Chaired Professor of Strategy and International Management at Insead in France.

JOHN P. KOTTER is the Konosuke Matsushita Professor of Leadership, Emeritus, at Harvard Business School.

LISA LASKOW LAHEY is the associate director of the Change Leadership Group at Harvard's Graduate School of Education.

MARTY LINSKY is a cofounder and partner at Cambridge Leadership Associates, a consulting firm in Boston.

RENÉE MAUBORGNE is the Insead Distinguished Fellow and a professor of strategy at Insead in France.

DEBRA E. MEYERSON is an associate professor of organizational behavior at Stanford University's School of Education.

NITIN NOHRIA is the dean of Harvard Business School.

MICHAEL A. ROBERTO is a professor of management at Bryant University in Smithfield, Rhode Island.

HAROLD L. SIRKIN is a Chicago-based senior partner and managing director at The Boston Consulting Group, a global management consulting firm.

THOMAS A. STEWART, formerly the editor of *Harvard Business Review,* is the chief marketing and knowledge officer at Booz & Company in New York.

BERT SPECTOR is an associate professor of organizational behavior at Northeastern University in Boston.

Index